Life Without Limits

Life

Without limits

Powerful Truths
That Bring Hope and Meaning

Clifford Goldstein

 REVIEW AND HERALD®
PUBLISHING ASSOCIATION
Since 1861 | www.reviewandherald.com

Published by Autumn House® Publishing, a division of Review and Herald® Publishing, Hagerstown, MD 21741-1119

Autumn House® titles may be purchased in bulk for educational, business, fund-raising, or sales promotional use. For information, please e-mail SpecialMarkets@reviewandherald.com.

Autumn House® Publishing publishes biblically based materials for spiritual, physical, and mental growth and Christian discipleship.

The author assumes full responsibility for the accuracy of all facts and quotations as cited in this book.

This book was
Edited by Gerald Wheeler
Copyedited by James Cavil
Designed by Trent Truman
Cover art ©Misha/123RF
Typeset: Galliard 11/14

Unless otherwise specified, Scripture quotations in this book are from the New King James Version. Copyright © 1979, 1980, 1982 by Thomas Nelson, Inc. Used by permission. All rights reserved.

Scripture quotations marked NASB are from the *New American Standard Bible,* copyright 1960, 1962, 1963, 1968, 1971, 1972, 1973, 1975, 1977, 1994 by The Lockman Foundation. Used by permission.

Bible texts in this book marked NIV are from the *Holy Bible, New International Version.* Copyright © 1973, 1978, 1984, International Bible Society. Used by permission of Zondervan Bible Publishers.

PRINTED IN U.S.A.

11 10 09 08 07   5 4 3 2 1

LCCN 2007022609

ISBN 978-0-8280-2059-6

CONTENTS

1

EINSTEIN'S BRAIN

STEALING EINSTEIN'S BRAIN

Everyone always wanted a piece of Albert Einstein (an interview, a quote, a signature, a memento, whatever), and that obsession with him didn't die when he did, either. So great was the mania for anything Einstein that between the man's death and burial his brain was snatched out of his head like a walnut out of its shell. The brain that had, for almost a half century, dominated physics disappeared like one of the subatomic particles that had so fascinated it.

One rumor said that someone had dissected

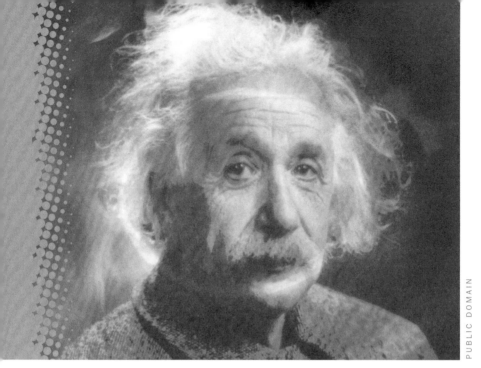

Albert Einstein reshaped our understanding of the universe.

the organ and stored it in a garage in Saskatchewan, next to hockey sticks and deflated basketballs. The truth, however, was that—after performing an autopsy on Einstein (who died of an aortic aneurysm) in 1955—the attending physician, Dr. Thomas Harvey, opened up the corpse's skull and removed the brain, ostensibly for medical research. The only problem was, the doctor took the brain and never returned it (supposedly, too, Einstein's ophthalmologist got the eyes, which he would on occasion take out and show around at parties).

"Harvey kept the brain himself," wrote a journalist about the fate of Einstein's brain, "not at the hospital but at home, and when he left Princeton he simply took it with him. Years passed. There were no studies or findings. And, in turn, no legal action was brought against Harvey, as there was no precedent in the courts for the recovery of a brain under such circumstances. And then Harvey fell off the radar screen. When he gave an occasional interview—in local newspaper articles from 1956 and 1979 and 1988—he always repeated that he was about 'a year from finishing study on the specimen.'"[1]

After holding on to "the specimen" for 40 years, and doing little with it but doling out small pieces to a select few, Dr. Harvey—whose practice sank after it became known what he had done (being a ghoul wasn't exactly a great medical career move)—made a decision. Now in his 80s and perhaps feeling guilty, he decided to give the brain back to the family, which meant an Einstein granddaughter living in Berkeley, California. Journalist Michael Paterniti, who befriended Dr. Harvey, offered to drive him from the East Coast to Einstein's granddaughter, and so off they went on a cross-country trip in a Buick Skylark with Einstein's formaldehyde-soaked brain floating in a Tupperware bowl in the trunk.

> They were holding in their hands the literal place that three centuries of Newtonian physics were overthrown.

Paterniti wrote a book, *Driving Mr. Albert,* that recounted one of the more unusual road trips in American history: an old guilty doctor, a gifted journalist, and, of course, Albert Einstein's brain sloshing in the trunk for about 3,000 miles, which (as one could imagine) caused spasms of hoopla along the way.

The most insightful scene, however, came toward the end of the trip, when the two men met Einstein's perplexed granddaughter, Evelyn. Although she knew that they were coming with her famous grandfather's brain, she wasn't quite sure what she was supposed to do with it. At one point Evelyn Einstein and Paterniti were sitting in the front seat of the Skylark when he opened the lid to show her Grandpa Albert's brain.

"I lift the lid, unravel a swath of damp cloth, and then maybe a dozen golf-ball-size chunks of the brain spill out—parts of the cerebral cortex and the frontal lobe," Paterniti wrote. "The smell of formaldehyde smacks us like a backhand. . . . The pieces are sealed in celloidin—the pinkish, liver-colored blobs of brain rimmed by gold wax. I pick some out of the plastic container and hand a few to

Evelyn. They feel squishy, weigh about the same as very light beach stones."

She and Paterniti passed pieces back and forth for a few more moments, and then Evelyn, who remembered her grandfather very well, looked up at Paterniti and said, "So this is what all the fuss is about?" A moment later she fondled another piece and commented, "You could make a nice necklace of this one."[2]

Then, calmly, quietly, they placed the pieces back into the Tupperware container and closed the lid on Albert Einstein's brain.

A Matter of Fact About the Fact of Matter

Put aside the weirdness of the scene (sitting in a car with Albert Einstein's granddaughter and passing around parts of his brain as if they were stolen jewels). Instead, consider the fact that they were holding in their hands the literal (and we mean *literal*) place that almost three centuries of Newtonian physics were overthrown. Within those "golf-ball-size chunks of the brain" the foundation of nuclear physics had been formulated. Somewhere right there, in those "pinkish, liver-colored blobs," the formula $E = mc^2$ emerged, a concept that changed the world. Those little pieces of matter (no longer gray but pink) pulled the theories of special and then general relativity out of the air, theories that showed that time and space were not absolute but change depending upon the amount of matter involved and the speed of the observer. In short, those few clumps of matter that they held in their hands while sitting in the front seat of a Buick Skylark on a street in Berkeley, California, had created some of the most fasci-

Journalist Michael Paterniti drove Dr. Harvey cross-country in a Buick Skylark to return Einstein's brain to the family.

nating and valuable ideas in the history of humanity.

Though the symbolism of the scene presents many possibilities, one is—Could Einstein, and all his genius, his ideas, his passions (Albert was somewhat of a Casanova), be limited to this brain matter, to those rills and crevices composed of neurons and fiber? Or, even, could it be restricted to just his entire physical structure—his brain and the rest of his body?

Is that, in the end, all Albert was?

Ultimately, what are any of us, really—purely physical beings, living by physical laws alone, exuding emotions, ideas, art, and creativity the way the stomach secretes peptic acid and the liver bile? Are we, and all that we do and think and create, nothing more than purely physical phenomena, nothing more than the motion of atoms, the synthesis of proteins, the binding or activation of adenylate cyclase, the sequence of ACTH, alpha-MSH, beta-MSH, and beta-lipotropin? Is the question of whom we'll marry merely different confluences of physical vectors? Could, ideally, everything about us—our thoughts, our desires, our choices—be explained, expressed, and predicted the same way that we can the motions of the stars?

The answer depends on one major question, and that involves our origins. How did we get here, and why? If we're the products of purely physical forces, within a purely physical universe—with nothing existing outside of matter and motion, nothing greater than matter and motion, nothing beyond matter and motion—then how could we be anything other than matter and motion? Could the whole ever be more than the sum of its parts? Of course not, some would argue. Thus, in this view, we are physical processes totally determined by antecedent physical

> Are we, and all that we do and think and create, nothing more than purely physical phenomena, nothing more than the motion of atoms?

activity, which means that we have no more free will than a windup doll or a computer running a program.

THE SENTENCE

A young man stood before the judge, who had just sentenced him to 10 years in prison. When asked if he had anything to say, the criminal said: "Yes, I do."

"OK," the magistrate responded, nodding, "go ahead."

"Judge," he asserted, approaching the bench, "how can you in good conscience sentence me to jail? It's not fair."

The judge dropped his reading glasses to the end of his nose, looked down at the defendant, and asked, "It's not?"

"No!"

"OK, explain."

"It's because," the man said, edging even closer, "from the moment I was born, from my family, from my genes, from my upbringing, from my environment, from my friends—everything predetermined me to a life of crime through no choice of my own. I couldn't have turned out any differently. I'm no more responsible for my actions than water is for flowing downstream. I had no choice for any of the things I did."

The judge sat there, silent, pondering. After a few moments he leaned forward and, speaking directly into the young man's face, said, "Well, son, I'll tell you how I can sentence you to 10 years in prison. From the moment I was born, from my family, my genes, my upbringing, my environment—everything that ever happened in my life has forced me, through no choice of my own, to sentence you to these 10 years."

The judge then slammed down his gavel, and a police officer took the prisoner away.

"Judge, how can you in good conscience sentence me to jail? It's not fair."

©PHOTODISC

ORGANIC ROBOTS

Are we, then, like that judge and criminal, so totally captive to physical forces that everything we do—from what we eat for breakfast to whom we love—are not really free choices but the inevitable outcome of what came before? However it might otherwise feel, are our "free choices" as predetermined as our DNA? "Everything that happens," wrote Arthur Schopenhauer, "from the largest to the smallest, happens necessarily."[3] If we take this purely materialistic view of reality, it's hard to believe otherwise.

On the other hand, if the idea of our existence as being nothing but the random motion of nonrational atoms seems about as adequate as love being nothing but hormonal excretions, then our origins must come from something greater than physical laws, something more than motion and matter. There would have to be a power greater than the mechanical and physical laws that run the universe, something that created not only those laws but along with them our freedom, our creativity, and our capacity to love—aspects of our existence that don't appear to be defined only by nature's laws.

And who else—or what else—could that power be, other than God, the Creator? When the Bible says that humanity was made "in the image of God" (Genesis 9:6), this could mean that things such as human freedom, creativity, and love are the manifestation of the character of God Himself. Again, if there is no God who has created a world in which free choice exists, one in

If there is no God who has created a world in which free choice exists, then it's hard to see ourselves as anything but organic robots hardwired with neurons instead of silicon chips.

© ISTOCKPHOTO.COM/A-PAPANTONIOU

12

which freedom functions at a level beyond the purely physical, then it's hard to see ourselves as anything but organic robots hardwired with neurons instead of silicon chips.

Which is it?

The answer's important because within it we can find meaning and purpose to our existence, if any exists at all. After all, it would be hard (though maybe not impossible) to discover much meaning and purpose were we nothing but matter and motion, beings with no control of our thoughts, actions, or choices. (It would be depressing, too, for if we are purely physical processes alone, then we have no choice but to imagine ourselves as free even though we're really not.) On the other hand, if we're beings created by a conscious force who has made us free and has given us the capacity to make choices on our own, then our lives can take on a whole new dimension, one infinitely beyond mere physical forces that can no more choose for themselves than the pages of a book can select the words that will go on it.

Are we mere automatons, or free beings created in the image of a loving God?

Again, which is it? Are we mere automatons, or free beings created in the image of a loving God?

This question is just another way of asking, Who are we? What are we? What do our lives mean? This book seeks, among other things, to look at these questions and—with logic, reason, and a measure of faith—provide a few answers.

And the great news, too, is that you don't need Einstein's brain to understand those answers, either.

---

[1] Michael Paterniti, *Driving Mr. Albert: A Trip Across America With Einstein's Brain* (New York: Random House, 2000), p. 24.

[2] *Ibid.*, p. 194.

[3] Arthur Schopenhauer, *Essay on the Freedom of the Will* (Mineola, N.Y.: Dover Publications, 2005), p. 62.

CLIFFORD'S PRINCIPLE

A QUESTION OF SCIENCE

ost people have never heard of Werner von Siemens. Many, though, recognize the name Siemens AG. Beginning in the 1840s as a little workshop in Berlin—which created the first long-distance telegraph line in Europe (about 300 miles [500 kilometers])—Siemens AG eventually burgeoned into one of the most innovative companies in the world. Creating about 8,200 inventions per year, Siemens AG is now a multibillion-dollar corporation. Present in more than 190 countries, the

PUBLIC DOMAIN

Werner von Siemens

Those who once envisioned endless scientific progress never imagined the threat of nuclear bombs.

company employs about 480,000 people, who produce all sorts of electronic equipment—everything from phones, to computers, to motors, to home appliances and hearing aids. More than likely, Siemens AG has touched your life in one way or another.

Werner von Siemens (1816-1892) was the genius who began the company. Toward the end of his life, before a group of scientists in Berlin during the final decade of the nineteenth century, this brilliant inventor and entrepreneur expressed his faith in the power of science and scientific discovery to improve the lot of humanity.

"Therefore, gentlemen," he declared, "we will not be shaken in our belief that our research and inventive activity leads mankind to higher levels of culture, ennobling it and making it more accessible to ideal aspirations, that the impending scientific age will diminish its hardships and it sickness, enhance its enjoyment of life, and make it better, happier, and more content with its fate. And even though we may not always see the road ahead clearly, the road leading to these better conditions, we will nevertheless hold on to our conviction that the light of truth we are exploring will not lead us astray, and that the wealth of power it brings to mankind cannot diminish it but is bound to elevate it to a higher level of existence."[1]

How accurate was Siemens' prediction? Has the "light of truth"— which he understood as scientific "research and inventive activity"— made humanity "better, happier, and more content with its fate"? Can we, now well into the twenty-first century, share the great optimism that science created for so many before the beginning of the twentieth?

What do you think? Though science has, in many ways, improved our lot, we're now in a century in which science— far from offering us the hope of a better future—can make that future look pretty scary. Amid all his exuberance, Herr von Siemens never heard of suitcase nukes, global warming, nuclear winter, dirty bombs, or bioterrorism. Science is probably more of a threat to our existence than a means to make it better.

"Our entire much-praised technological progress, and civilization generally," Albert Einstein wrote, "could be compared to an axe in the hand of a pathological criminal."[2]

An axe? (He said that in 1917.) How about a 20-megaton thermonuclear device? *And a pathological criminal?* How about a religious fanatic instead?

©PHOTODISC

WHEN THEY BURNED BRUNO

Also, for all the hope it supposedly offers, science has been unable to answer the hardest and most fundamental questions about life. What is our purpose here? What reasons do we have for living? What is the meaning of life? of death? How can we find happiness? How should we act? What is moral or immoral? What does the future hold? Science might be able to help keep those who are dying alive a bit longer, but it offers no answers to why we shouldn't pull the plug. As Austrian philosopher Ludwig Wittgenstein has observed: "We feel that when all *possible* scientific questions have been answered, the problems of life remain completely untouched."[3]

If science cannot provide answers, where do we find them? Are we just fated to live our existence—spasms of cellular metabolism capable of contemplating the idea of eternity—only to vanish like vapor on a window, so that when we're gone it will be almost as if we never were here to begin with?

Polish poet Czeslaw Milosz caught the fleeting nature of our lives when he wrote:

"On this same square
they burned Giordano Bruno.
Henchman kindled the pyre
close-pressed by the mob.
Before the flames had died,
the taverns were full again,
baskets of olives and lemons
again on the vendors' shoulders."[4]

Who are we, and how are we—hemmed in by the eternity that came before us, oppressed by the thought of the one looming afterward, and surrounded by infinity on every side—supposed to make sense of it all? Can we have certain answers, or do we just go on guessing, conjecturing about the most important questions of life, only to have it all end in an eternal death? Science doesn't answer those questions for us. It doesn't even come close.

Yet answers are out there, answers to questions about the purpose and meaning of our existence, about how we should live, about death, about suffering, and about the future. Answers full of hope that take us beyond what we can see or ever figure out on our own through test tubes, field experiments, and computer-generated mathematical equations.

CLIFFORD'S PRINCIPLE

And not only are answers out there. You can have good reasons for believing them, too.

A story tells about a ship owner in the 1800s getting ready to send a vessel filled with emigrant families out to sea, families determined to start a new existence for themselves in a new world. The ship itself was somewhat old, quite battered, creaky, and prone to leak. And no wonder—it had crossed the ocean many times, weathering lots of North Atlantic storms. It was, the owner knew, in need of a number of repairs. Perhaps it would even require an overhauling, at least down the road. A few contractors and shipbuilders had suggested to him that it was not seaworthy, at least not without some serious work, but the ship owner knew that they had a vested interest in telling him just

A crumbling sailing ship left port with passengers seeking better lives in a new world.

that. After all, they were the ones who did the repair work on his ships, so of course they were going to tell him it should have some overhauling. Some of the crew members expressed a few words of concern, but the ship owner just dismissed them as idle chatter. Uneducated sailors— what did they know about the structure and engineering of a ship?

It is immoral to hold any view, even a correct one, based on flimsy evidence.

Sure, the boat had some problems, he told himself, but it was a sturdy old thing, had gone through some brutal storms before, and he had no real reason to think it couldn't handle one more. If he could get a few more runs out of it, then he'd be in financial shape to give it a good going-over. He just couldn't afford it now, and besides, it really didn't need it. The lingering doubts that remained he scuttled with the thought that in the end Providence would get this ship through because, after all, it was filled with hundreds of people seeking a better life elsewhere.

Yes, the ship owner said to himself, especially after he had uttered a few prayers in behalf of the ship and passengers, it would be safe. Standing in the harbor on a warm spring morning, he watched, peacefully and happily, as the ship sailed over the horizon.

"In such ways he acquired a sincere and comfortable conviction that his vessel was thoroughly safe and seaworthy; he watched her departure with a light heart, and benevolent wishes for the success of the exiles in their strange new home that was to be; and he got his insurance money when she went down in midocean and told no tales."[5]

The point of the story, told by a British philosopher named W. K. Clifford, was that people needed valid reasons for their beliefs, and that it was immoral to hold any view, even a correct one, based on flimsy evidence. If someone had the capacity and the opportunity to get enough information in order to form a belief, then it was incumbent upon that person to do just that. Otherwise that individual stood at great moral fault for holding his or her belief, again regardless of whether it was true or false.

ONCE DONE, DONE FOREVER

"Let us alter the case a little," Clifford continued, "and suppose that the ship was not unsound after all; that she made her voyage safely, and many others after it. Will that diminish the guilt of her owner? Not one jot. When an action is once done, it is right or wrong forever; no accidental failure of its good or evil fruits can possibly alter that. The man would not have been innocent; he would only have been not found out. The question of right or wrong has to do with the origin of his belief, not the matter of it; not what it was, but how he got it; not whether it turned out to be true or false, but whether he had a right to believe on such evidence as was before him."[6]

> Clifford's principle: "It is always wrong, everywhere, and for anyone, to believe anything upon insufficient evidence."

In the end, he summed up his position (known as Clifford's principle): "It is always wrong, everywhere, and for anyone, to believe anything upon insufficient evidence."[7]

We agree. Hence, *Life Without Limits*. It doesn't just express certain beliefs, but seeks to provide—for anyone, everywhere—sufficient evidence for them as well.

---

[1] In Rüdiger Safranski, *Martin Heidegger: Between Good and Evil* (Cambridge, Mass.: Harvard University Press, 1998), p. 35.

[2] In Alan Lightman, *A Sense of the Mysterious* (New York: Vintage Books, 2006), p. 110.

[3] Ludwig Wittgenstein, *Tractatus Logico-Philosophicus* (Atlantic Highlands, N.J.: Humanities Press International, 1961), p. 73.

[4] Czeslaw Milosz, "Campo dei Fiori," *New and Collected Poems* (New York: HarperCollins, 2003), p. 33.

[5] Quoted in *Philosophy of Religion*, ed. Charles Taliaferro and Paul Griffiths (Oxford, Eng.: Blackwell Publishing, 2003), p. 196.

[6] *Ibid.*

[7] *Ibid.*, p. 199.

THE BIG FREEZE
(or the Big Crunch)

CHOOSE YOUR ENDING

In Mongolia a boiler blew up. The explosion hurled the chunk of steaming steel over a six-story building. It then plummeted down on a white-haired old man who—having managed to make it through World War II, the Communist takeover, and the Cultural Revolution—didn't survive the boiler landing on his head.

In the United States a young man working for a newspaper went to get a photograph of a lad shot dead earlier that day during a drug deal. *A stranger*

©ISTOCKPHOTO.COM/ZOOMSTUDIO

The universe is filled with unnumbered clusters of stars known as galaxies.

coming to a house, knocking on the door, and asking for a photo of their dead 17-year-old in order that other strangers could put the picture in the newspaper so that even more strangers could gawk at it for a few seconds before using it to wrap fish, to build a fire, or to clean windows?

He wasn't expecting the warmest reception.

And he didn't get one (or the picture, either). As the young man was leaving, the dead boy's older brother stood by the door. Fulminating with pain over his sibling's troubled life—and death—he blurted out, "All that for nothing!"

For nothing? And the old man killed by the boiler? For nothing? What about any of us? Whether we live long and prosperously or expire as a mere child, what do we leave behind in the end but a corpse? Or, at best, we leave behind only those who—before becoming corpses themselves—will leave behind others who, before becoming corpses, will leave behind those who, before becoming corpses . . . and on and on.

"The Milky Way," wrote British physicist and astrobiologist Paul

Davies, "blazes with the light of a hundred billion stars, and every one of them is doomed. In ten billion years, most that we see now will have faded from sight, snuffed out from lack of fuel. . . . The universe, currently aglow with the prolific energy of nuclear power, will eventually exhaust this valuable resource. The era of light will be over forever."[1]

If, when the "era of light" ends and the big freeze begins, it will be as if we had never been, why bother being at all?

THE BIG CRUNCH

Not all scientists, however, expect the universe to vanish in the big freeze. They're anticipating the big crunch instead, when gravity pulls all matter together and everything collapses into a super-hot glob of dense material about the size of an atom.

In 1967 science fiction author Poul Anderson wrote *Tau Zero*, a novel about the big crunch. In his story the starship *Leonora Christine* careens across the cosmos, moving at velocities near the speed of light. Now, as Einstein's brain ("the pinkish, liver-colored blobs" we looked at in chapter 1) proved, the closer we move toward the speed of light, the slower time progresses for us. (Remember that famous thought experiment about twins? One twin goes off in a rocket that travels near the speed of light while the other stays on earth. The twin on earth waits 20 years for the spaceship to return, and when it does, her twin walks down the ramp and is only two years older than when she left, because, at the speed she traveled, time slowed for her, and so she aged only two years while her twin on earth aged 20.)

Well, the *Leonora Christine* travels so fast, and time slows down so

As a spaceship approaches the speed of light, time slows down for those traveling in it.

much, that what's minutes to them on board the ship are eons to those on earth. Then, unfortunately, the ship hits some interstellar dust that destroys the engine's decelerator, and the *Leonora* goes faster and faster, until it almost reaches the speed of light, *tau zero*. Those on board watch helplessly as time, for them, almost stops (according to Einstein, time ceases at the speed of light) while outside billions of years pass in what to the ship is just hours. Then, to their utter horror, the universe starts folding back upon itself in the big crunch. Temperatures rise, galaxies fold in on themselves, and the crew knows that it's only a matter of minutes

> **Poet Robert Frost once wrote about the world ending by either fire or ice.**

before they get swallowed up and incinerated in this tiny cosmic glob of super-dense matter the size of an atom.

Now (you'll be happy to know), the crew members of the *Leonora Christine* do find a way to escape. We, though, might not be so fortunate, which means that however the universe ends—the big crunch, the big freeze, or, as some anticipate, "the big rip"—we're all goners. Poet Robert Frost once wrote about the world ending by either fire or ice. Whether through fire, ice, crunch, a rip in the fabric of space, or cosmic freeze—everything we've ever did, thought, dreamed about, or accomplished will be forever gone and forgotten.

DEATH, THE GREAT ROBBER

Of course, we don't need to anticipate that last extinct star or the big crunch before we wonder about our long-term prospects. Death seems to rob life of every meaning we try to primp it with. "Once a man has realized," Leo Tolstoy observed, "that death is the end of everything, then there is nothing worse than life either."[2] However exaggerated, his point's nevertheless well taken. What's the purpose of anything that does not last, whose impact, influence, even memory, will be eternally forgotten, because eventually nothing that can remember it will exist? What means the life of a 6-month-old African baby who starves to death on a dehydrated breast in a doomed universe?

South American Jorge Luis Borges wrote about a hoodlum named Otálora who joins a Uruguayan gang. Otálora—seeking to usurp the leader, Bandeira—slowly starts taking his power, his authority, even his woman. Only at the last moment, before Bandeira has him shot, does Otálora see what has really happened.

> **"More than 50 percent of the finest household dust is made up of flakes of skin."**

"Otálora realizes, before he dies, that he has been betrayed from the beginning, that he has been sentenced to death, that he has been allowed to love, to command, and win because he was already as good as dead, because so far as Bandeira was concerned, he was already a dead man."[3]

Even if we get to love, to gain power, and to succeed in life (though so often we don't get any of this), each of us, like Otálora, is, in a sense, "already a dead man." It just happens sooner to some than others, that's all.

"More than 50 percent of the finest household dust is made up of flakes of skin," Midas Dekkers wrote. "If you think you're losing yourself, just look on top of the cupboard: run a finger across it and you'll be standing face to face with the state in which you'll find yourself in only a few decades' time. One slap of your hand on the mattress and you'll be flurrying about in the air."[4]

Is this life, with all its toils, struggles, and disappointments, the sum of all that we are, or could be? And then, to top it off, our

©PHOTODISC

often sad and miserable trek here—punctuated with a few lines, para-graphs, or pages of happiness (if lucky)—ends as dust that will itself collapse in the big crunch.

Is this our fate?

It depends . . .

[1] Paul Davies, *The Last Three Minutes* (New York: Perseus Books, 1994), pp. 49, 50.

[2] Leo Tolstoy, in a letter in the introduction to *Anna Karenin* (New York: Penguin Classics, 1978).

[3] Jorge Luis Borges, "The Dead Man," *The Aleph* (London: Penguin Classics, 2000), p. 25.

[4] Midas Dekkers, *The Way of All Flesh* (London: Harvill Press, 1997), p. 186.

4

ZEBRA
IN THE KITCHEN

THE LADY AND THE TIGER

In the previous chapter we left off with the idea that the pur-

pose of our lives depends upon something.

But upon what?

On how we got here, what else? As the oak's in the acorn, so

our end's in our beginning.

And what does that mean?

Two primary overarching views

of human origins exist. The first sees the

universe, and everything in it, as a product of purely material things

If you find a zebra in your kitchen, ignoring it will not make it go away.

that arose by chance. Everything—from the Andromeda Galaxy to our deepest longings—has a materialist origin and existence and consists of atoms and nothing more. All that exists is what some ancient materialists called "atoms and the void."

Modern materialists describe this position in the following way. About 15 billion years ago a tremendous explosion brought forth matter, energy, time, and space all at once, an event they call the big bang. Atoms created in this explosion formed gaseous clouds that coalesced into stars, and amid this interstellar panoply of light and heat molten globules cooled and hardened into the planets, including ours—third orb out. After billions of years, pools of water filled with increasingly complex chemicals. Simple life forms emerged from a mix of amino acids, and they evolved over eons into humans beings.

The crucial point is that these processes had no purpose, no intention, no goals, beginning with the big bang itself. They just happened. "Our universe," one scientist commented, "is simply one of those things which happen from time to time."[1]

If this view is correct, then our end (and our middle, too)—all of which comes out of our origins—is as dismal as suggested above. Our existence has no purpose. Because the original mix had no goals or intent, the final product contains none. We're just one of those things that occurs from time to time. As a jack-in-the-box pops out of the box only because something put it in there to begin with, if whatever made us has no meaning, then none can come out of the box with us.

In a famous quote reflecting this view, French biologist Jacques Monod wrote: "The ancient covenant is in pieces; man knows at last that he is alone in the universe's unfeeling immensity, out of which he emerged only by chance. His destiny is nowhere spelled out, nor is his duty. The kingdom above or the darkness below; it is for him to choose."[2]

One wonders, though, where we would find a "kingdom above" in Monod's chance cosmos.

Nineteenth-century author Frank Stockton wrote about a king with a weird sense of justice. He would have male offenders placed in a room that had only two closed doors leading out—one opened to a woman, the other to a tiger. Those on trial didn't know which was which. If they chose the door

©PHOTODISC/ISTOCKPHOTO.COM/GLOBALP

What lies behind life's doors?

with the woman, they'd be deemed innocent and not only set free but given the woman. But if they wound up with the tiger, they'd be deemed guilty and eaten alive by the beast.

The characters in Stockton's short story had at least one good option. Monod's universe doesn't, it would seem, offer even one, unless his "kingdom above" actually existed. It's hard, though, to imagine where it would be in a universe that had no meaning.

FROZEN HEADS

Along this same line of thought, some say that our existence is like the toss of dice. Not quite, though. After all, dice do have a purpose. The numbers on them were specifically and consciously arranged a certain way, and they get thrown with a specific intent in mind. In the present scientific view our existence, our lives, our hopes, and our dreams all came into being without any purposes in mind, because there was no mind to purpose them.

In this view more thought lies behind someone scratching their initials into wet cement or spraying graffiti on a wall than went into the creation of the world.

We are a chance system of chemical reactions, nothing more. Whether Bach writing a symphony or a plant doing photosynthesis, both are simply different kinds of molecular processes (a confluence of atoms, and a chance one at that), and the same mindless forces that brought these atomic processes here will eventually take them away.

Disturbed by the implications of this purely materialistic worldview, some have put their hope in cryonics, in which technicians place the dead in vats of liquid nitrogen and keep them in cold storage. The idea is that perhaps science will advance far enough so that it can thaw out the bodies and bring them back to life. Others—believing that in about 7 billion years the sun will explode and swallow up the earth—warn that we must therefore colonize space. Yet when the universe burns out, or collapses on itself, it's going to take our all interstellar colonies and thawed-out flesh with it, so a lot of good either option will do us in the long run.

In short, the prevailing scientific view of our origins leaves us with little to hope beyond our flimsy and uncertain existence here. As the twentieth century's leading atheist expressed it: "All the labors of the ages, all the devotion, all the inspiration, all the noonday brightness of human genius . . . the whole temple of man's achievements must inevitably be buried beneath the debris of a universe in ruins."[3]

> **"The whole temple of man's achievements must inevitably be buried beneath the debris of a universe in ruins."**

So, to return to our questions: "Is this life, with all its toils, struggles, and disappointments, the sum of all that we are, or could be? And then, to top it off, the often sad and miserable story of our lives—punctuated with a few lines, or paragraphs, or pages of happiness (if lucky)—ends as dust? Is this our fate?"

Yes, if the above view of our origins is correct.

On the other hand . . .

THE GOD HYPOTHESIS

On the other hand, what?

On the other hand, we have another overarching view of our origins, one that encompasses a perspective grander and broader than the narrow confines of the scientific materialistic one. This other position argues that everything created came from a Creator—from a God (or gods) who brought everything into existence. In this view we're here not by chance, but for a purpose, and we can divine some of those intents through the creation, which itself testifies to the existence of God. After all, just as a painting implies a painter, doesn't a creation imply a Creator?

"As flies to wanton boys are we to th' gods."—William Shakespeare

Of course, even then our fate may be far from secure. A malicious being, or beings, could have put us all here with the intent of making us miserable. "As flies to wanton boys are we to th' gods," said Shakespeare's Gloucester. "They kill us for their sport."[4] Or He (She? It? They?) could have created and then orphaned us here. The idea of a deity, in and of itself, doesn't automatically offer more hope than does the purely materialistic worldview. Deity, in fact, could render our fate worse, for instead of us expiring into eternity (as the atheistic position implies), we could be cast into an eternal burning hell, or reincarnated as galley slaves on a Phoenician trireme in a parallel universe somewhere.

In contrast, the idea of a Creator, particularly a loving one, opens up a whole new realm of hope, of something beyond the hopelessness of the modern scientific worldview, in which destruction ends a universe that lacked purpose to begin with. "Only God, it seems to me, can take from death the last word," Eng lish author John Polkinghorne observed. "If the human intuition of hope—that all will be well, that the world makes ultimate sense—is not a vain delusion, then God must exist."[5]

The atheistic materialistic view offers no possibility of any future other than that of cold dust drifting through a worn-out cosmos. Deity alone offers us the *possibility* of more. Again, a God's no guarantee of a good end, only the *possibility* of one. In contrast, the scientific worldview guarantees us only a death much longer than whatever precedes it. "It's not that life is so short," a T-shirt declares, "it's just that death is so long."

Our most pressing and important question, then, deals with origins—for only in how we began can we find the answers about our life and, even more important, about our end. Just as the color of our eyes originates in our genes, our ends originate in our beginnings. "As our fate is totally dependent upon the matrix that produced and sustains us," Huston Smith commented, "interest in its nature is the holiest interest that can visit us."[6]

What produced us? What sustains us? Purposeless, cold forces—or deity of one kind or another? Are we here alone, or does God exist? And if so, does this God come "only in silent shadows and in dreams,"[7] or can we know more about Him?

As stated before, this book seeks to make Clifford's principle—"It is always wrong, everywhere and for anyone, to believe anything upon insufficient evidence"—its own.

Of the two options, then, which one follows it better?

ZEBRA IN THE KITCHEN

Suppose one day you came home and found a massive zebra drinking out of your kitchen sink. Surprised, you ask your spouse (or whomever you live with), "Where did this zebra come from?"

"It came from nothing," the other person responds.

From *nothing*?

Ridiculous! Why? Because nothing comes from nothing. The old Latin phrase *ex nihilo nihil fit* ("Out of nothing, nothing comes") is

It's not that life is so short, it's just that death is so long

an obvious first principle, a truth too basic even to debate. How could anything arise from nothing? Zebras (whether in the jungle or in the kitchen) must originate from something, not from "nothing," because "out of nothing, nothing comes." It would be easier to get six out of three than to get something—anything—out of nothing.

Then what about the earth, the sky, the stars? Or you, your shoes, your mother? Certainly they, like the zebra, couldn't have come from "nothing," could they? Anything created, anything that once was not but came to be, did so only by something other than itself, by something previous to it. The shoemaker obviously existed prior to your shoe.

Now, for many years people believed that the universe was eternal. Being uncreated, it had always existed. There was never a time when the universe was not. Despite the difficult philosophical questions such a position raised, it removed the need of a Creator. The universe didn't have a Creator because, always existing, it didn't require one.

Scientists now believe, however, that the universe was not eternal, but had a beginning. Yes, at some point in the past, it did *not* exist. Stephen Hawking, perhaps the greatest scientist since Einstein, wrote that "almost everyone now believes that the universe, and time itself, had a beginning at the big bang."[8] Like your shoe, the universe wasn't always there.

The conclusion that the universe had a beginning leads to the obvious question: If the universe had a starting point, then what or who set it in motion? If it's absurd to believe that a zebra in your kitchen came from nothing, how much more so to believe that the universe—and all that it contains (ourselves and zebras included)—did as well. Therefore, before the big bang, before the universe was, something had to already be—something powerful enough to set in motion the forces that led to life on earth, not to mention the ex-

Stephen Hawking

istence of billions of galaxies and stars. And other than God, who, or what, could that be, because who, or what, could have created the universe?

Once scientists agreed that the universe came into being at some time or another, they forced upon themselves the inescapable question of God. As Hawking conceded: "So long as the universe had a beginning, we could suppose it had a creator."[9]

THE NOTHING ARGUMENT

"Suppose" is right. The implications surrounding a created universe point so strongly to God that some scientists have been compelled by the obvious to embrace the absurd. Instead of God being the creator of the universe, they argue that "nothing" was the creator.

Nothing?

That's what some are saying.

"Conceivably," physicist Alan Guth suggested, "*everything* can be created from nothing. And 'everything' might include a lot more than we can see. . . . It is fair to say that the universe is the ultimate free lunch."[10]

> "Conceivably, *everything* can be created from nothing."

How is "nothing" able to create "everything"?

Through quantum fluctuations, some scientists theorize. Huh?

Quantum fluctuations are complicated physical processes that, supposedly, created the universe. If so, that theory begs the question. Where did the laws of physics (much less the energy) needed to produce those quantum fluctuations come from?

As one critic mocks: "Alan Guth writes in pleased astonishment that the universe did arise from 'essentially . . . nothing at all': as it happens, a false vacuum patch '10^{-26} centimeters in diameter' and '10^{-32} solar masses.' It would appear, then, that 'essentially nothing' has both spatial extension and mass. While these facts may strike Guth as inconspicuous, others may suspect that nothingness, like death, is not a matter of degrees."[11]

Or, as another critic of this everything-out-of-nothing hypothesis remarks: "How do we account for the situation within which one or more gigantic quantum fluctuations could occur? The atheist says we just have to assume it and treat it as a given."[12]

All the scientific intricacies and nuances of quantum fluctuations aside, the critics' points are well taken. Whatever a quantum fluctuation is supposed to be, it's certainly not "nothing." It has mass, energy, and physical laws, and these things—like the zebra in your kitchen—had to come from somewhere.

The question, again, is: From where?

©PHOTODISC

WHICH IS MORE REASONABLE?

Of the two positions—that the universe was created by "nothing," or that it's the result of a powerful God—which remains more logical, more reasonable? Which better fits the evidence: All that exists (stars, clouds, people, trees, etc.) sprang from "nothing," or came from a Creator? Is it sensible to accept as a given the physical processes needed for quantum fluctuations, or to acknowledge a creator God, one who always existed?

Nothing as creator is, really, the only logical option for the atheist. Why? Because if something other than an eternal God—that is, a God who always existed—made the universe, then whatever it was, it had to be created by something before it, which had to be originated by something before it . . . and on and on endlessly.

"In the beginning *God* created the heavens and the earth" (Genesis 1:1). Or was it "In the beginning *nothing* created the heavens and the earth"?

Thus the universe could never have had a starting point. It would have to be, like God, from eternity. But the universe doesn't endlessly go back in time. Once it just wasn't there. And because there was a time that the universe did not exist, something obviously had to start it, and who or what could that be, other than God?

Unless, of course, *nothing* created it?

"In the beginning *God* created the heavens and the earth" (Genesis 1:1). Or was it "In the beginning *nothing* created the heavens and the earth"?

Which better fits Clifford's principle?

Take your pick.

[1] In Dennis Richard Danielson, ed., *The Book of the Cosmos* (Cambridge, Mass.: Perseus Publishing, 2000), p. 482.

[2] http://dannyreviews.com/h/Chance_and_Necessity.html.

[3] Bertrand Russell, *Why I Am Not a Christian* (New York: Simon and Schuster, 1957), p. 107.

[4] William Shakespeare, *King Lear*, Act IV, scene 1, lines 36, 37.

[5] John Polkinghorne, *Belief in God in an Age of Science* (New Haven, Conn.: Yale University Press, 1998), p. 21.

[6] Huston Smith, *Beyond the Post-Modern Mind* (Wheaton, Ill.: Theosophical Publishing House, 1992), p. 53.

[7] Wallace Stevens, "Sunday Morning," *The Collected Poems* (New York: Vintage Books, 1990), p. 67.

[8] Stephen Hawking and Roger Penrose, *The Nature of Space and Time* (Princeton, N.J.: Princeton University Press, 1996), p. 20.

[9] Stephen Hawking, *A Brief History of Time* (New York: Bantam Books, 1988), pp. 140, 141.

[10] In Danielson, p. 483.

[11] *Ibid.*, p. 495.

[12] Ian Barbour, *When Science Meets Religion* (San Francisco: HarperSanFrancisco, 2000), p. 44.

WHISTLING
SHRIMP

GAS RAID FROM MARS

*I*n 2005 Hollywood produced *War of the Worlds*, starring Tom Cruise in a remake of H. G. Wells' novel about an invasion from outer space. The movie, though, didn't cause the hoopla that the radio version did in 1938, when—hearing it drama-tized over the air—thousands actually believed that creatures from Mars had landed in New Jersey. Those who missed the opener ("The Columbia Broadcasting System and its affiliated stations present

PUBLIC DOMAIN

H. G. Wells

Could there be a whole world filled with whistling shrimp?

Orson Welles and the Mercury Theatre on the Air in 'The War of the Worlds,' by H. G. Wells") heard only a dramatic account of a Martian attack: "Ladies and gentlemen, here is the latest bulletin from the Intercontinental Radio News. Toronto, Canada: Professor Morse of McMillan University reports observing a total of three explosions on the planet Mars, between the hours of 7:45 p.m. and 9:20 p.m., Eastern Standard Time. This confirms earlier reports received from American observatories.

"Now, nearer home, comes a special bulletin from Trenton, New Jersey. It is reported that at 8:50 p.m. a huge, flaming object, believed to be a meteorite, fell on a farm in the neighborhood of Grovers Mill, New Jersey, 22 miles from Trenton.

"The flash in the sky was visible within a radius of several hundred miles and the noise of the impact was heard as far north as Elizabeth.

"We have dispatched a special mobile unit to the scene, and will have our commentator, Carl Phillips, give you a word picture of the scene as soon as he can reach there from Princeton.

"In the meantime, we take you to the Hotel Martinet in Brooklyn, where Bobby Millette and his orchestra are offering a program of dance music."

As the broadcast progressed, the correspondent reached Grovers Mill and, instead of a meteorite, he saw a giant cylinder that had landed in the field. Something then started to crawl out of the top, and Carl Phillips described it: "Something's wriggling out of the shadow like a gray snake. Now it's another one, and another one, and another one! They look like tentacles to me. I can see the thing's body now. It's large, large as a bear, and it glistens like wet leather. But that face, it— Ladies and gentlemen, it's indescribable. I can hardly force myself to keep looking at it—so awful. The eyes are black and gleam like a serpent. The mouth is V-shaped with saliva dripping from its rimless lips that seem to quiver and pulsate. The monster or whatever it is can hardly move. It seems weighed down by . . . possibly gravity or something. The thing's . . . rising up now, and the crowd falls back now. They've seen plenty. This is the most extraordinary experience, ladies and gentlemen. I can't find words . . . I'll pull this microphone with me as I talk. I'll have to stop the description until I can take a new position. Hold on, will you please, I'll be right back in a minute . . . We are bringing you an eyewitness account of what's happening on the Wilmuth farm, Grovers Mill, New Jersey."

Not knowing that it was only a dramatization, panicked Americans fled into the streets or into air-raid shelters. The New York *Times* the next day described what happened: "A wave of mass hysteria seized thousands of radio listeners between 8:15

Tripod from *War of the Worlds,* by H. G. Wells.

and 9:30 last night when a broadcast of a dramatization of H. G. Wells' fantasy, 'The War of the Worlds,' led thousands to believe that an interplanetary conflict had started with invading Martians spreading wide death and destruction in New Jersey and New York. . . . In Newark, in a single block at Heddon Terrace and Hawthorne Avenue, more than 20 families rushed out of their houses with wet handkerchiefs and towels over their faces to flee from what they believed was to be a gas raid. Some began moving household furniture.

If you leave out God, you need something more than chance alone to explain it. So why not space aliens?

"Throughout New York families left their homes, some to flee to nearby parks. Thousands of persons called the police, newspapers, and radio stations here and in other cities of the United States and Canada seeking advice on protective measures against the raids."[1]

Invaders from outer space? Sounds kind of corny today. Yet some scientists are using a similar argument to account for the existence of life on earth. And that's because if you leave out God, you need something more than chance alone to explain it.

So why not space aliens?

THE SPACE-INVADER HYPOTHESIS

As we've been saying, the common scientific model hypothesizes that we came to exist by nothing but a chance grouping of matter and energy.

"With this single argument," zoologist E rnst Haeckel wrote many years ago, "the mystery of the universe is explained, the Deity annulled, and a new era of infinite knowledge ushered in."[2]

Not so fast, Ernst. During the past century (Haeckel died in

©PHOTODISC

Did alien spaceships first bring life to earth?

1919), scientists have been finding such complexity within the universe, such an incredibly finely tuned balance of forces essential to human life, that it's more likely for rain falling on a keyboard to type out *The Iliad* in Greek, Latin, and Finnish than for chance alone to produce our existence. Chance explains the complexity found in nature about as well as *nothing* accounts for the zebra in the kitchen.

Faced with these facts, scientists and thinkers have found themselves forced to create other models. One recent idea, which found its way into *Time* magazine, asserts that "our universe might have been manufactured by a race of superintelligent extraterrestrial beings."[3] Francis Crick (one of the codiscoverers of the structure of DNA) pushed a different theory: intelligent beings from another galaxy sent spaceships to seed the earth with life. God didn't make us—aliens did. Crick wasn't your everyday late-night radio talk show loony, either. A revered scientific researcher, he won a Nobel prize in 1962 for his work on DNA.

"And thus," as one incredulous writer expressed it, "the Nobel prize winner embraced the theory that space aliens sent rocket ships to seed the earth."[4]

Maybe those Martians from the H. G. Wells story were coming back to see how well their seedlings were faring . . .

THE MANY-UNIVERSES HYPOTHESIS

Another view, one that has been (somewhat at least) well received by the scientific community, goes by the title "many-universes hypothesis." It claims that there exists a very large—perhaps infinite—number of universes besides our own. Ours, the one in which we live and that contains the galaxies we scan with the Hubble telescope, is just one among billions. Most of these other universes, the theory suggests, don't have the incredible fine-tuning needed for life to exist, so most (unlike ours) are lifeless.

However (and here's the point), if instead of one universe, there are billions, maybe even an infinite number, then the chance of one of them being finely tuned for life becomes less incredible. Such billions of other universes greatly increase the odds that one of them will have the many incredible variables needed to sustain life.

©PHOTODISC

Look at it like this: If you flip five coins one time each, what are the odds of all five coming up heads? Certainly not as good as the odds of getting five heads in a row *if you flip 10 million coins* one time each. You're much more likely, at some point along the way, to get five in a row by tossing 10 million coins than by tossing just five. That's what the many-universes hypothesis is about: the more times you have to try something, the greater chance you have of getting it. So the more universes out there, the greater the odds of one of them turning out like the incredibly intricate one that we live in.

If you flip five coins one time each, what are the odds of all five coming up heads?

THE BLACK-HOLE HYPOTHESIS

Of course, one may humbly ask, "Where did all these universes, including our own, come from?" Well, scientists have a few theories about that as well.

One theory proposes that black holes—those mysterious entities whose gravitational pull is so strong that they allow nothing, not even light, to escape—could be the engine that forms new universes. Somehow, by tearing and rearranging the fabric of space-time, black holes create new universes, whose own black holes in turn produce more new universes, and on and on forever.

Another theory, based on the idea of "inflationary cosmology," hypothesizes that a small section of space underwent an enormous expansion that allows more and more space to form, and from this constant expansion of space more and more universes arise.

Though other scientific theories exist, they have one thing in

©PHOTODISC/DIGITALLY MODIFIED

Do black holes rip the fabric of space and create new universes?

> **Scientific theories attempt to explain the incredible complexity of the universe without recourse to what to some would seem the most obvious explanation— a Creator or a Designer.**

common, and that is that they attempt to explain the incredible design and complexity of the universe without recourse to what to some would seem the most obvious explanation—a Creator or a Designer.

After all, who needs God when you've got space aliens and black holes?

But think a moment. Which makes better sense?

"*God*, who made the world and everything in it" (Acts 17:24)?

"*Black holes*, which made the world and everything in it"?

Or "*Space aliens*, who made the world and everything in it"?

(And don't forget Clifford's principle, either, as you decide.)

WHISTLING SHRIMP

Before you do, consider the following . . .

As might be expected, some find these explanations for human life (aliens, black holes, etc.) unsatisfactory. For starters, in the case of the many-universes hypothesis, no one has ever seen or detected even one of these supposed universes, much less multiple ones. Their existence is pure speculation.

"Belief in multiple universes," cosmologist George E llis comments, "is just as much a matter of faith as any other religious belief."[5]

In fact, arguing for an infinite number of universes allows anything to be explained. Why not speculate that among these universes one is made only of jelly beans, or that in another men have babies, women grow beards, and shrimp whistle Brahms? The rationality behind the many-worlds hypothesis is, in a sense, a forfeiture of rational thinking itself.

Besides, though proposed as alternatives to God, such theories merely push the parameters back, that's all. If aliens created our universe or seeded the planet, that's fine. But who or what created those aliens? And even if black holes produce other universes, where did the first black hole—and all the physical laws governing it—come from? Or where did the original matter, energy, and complicated physical laws needed for cosmic inflation first arise?

THIRTY-MAN FIRING SQUAD

Others argue that because we as humans could not exist in a universe incapable of the incredible complexity and fine-tuning needed to produce us, it's no big deal that we're here. The universe had to create us in order for us to be here and marvel at its wonders to begin with. However, far from answering the question about the mind-boggling balance of factors that made life possible, that argument ignores it. It's as if a prisoner facing a 30-man firing squad from five meters away goes free because all 30 fire and miss, and then announces, "Of course they had to miss— otherwise I wouldn't be here to talk about it. Nothing extraordinary here."

Is the spontaneous origin of life as probable as someone surviving a 30-man firing squad?

During the eighteenth century—long before science uncovered the kind of complexity in nature that has caused such a shift today in our understanding about origins— British philosopher David Hume challenged the idea that creation reveals the God of Scripture. Though conceding (through the mouth of a person engaged in a dialogue) an intricacy and design in nature "to a degree beyond what human senses and faculties can trace and explain"[6] (again, when he wrote no one had ever heard of DNA, much less even

David Hume

begun exploring any of the stunning intricacies of the cell), Hume fought hard to dismiss the idea of a Creator behind it all. Ultimately, though, he had to argue that "matter may contain the source or spring of order originally, within itself . . . ; and . . . that the several elements, from an internal unknown cause, may fall into the most exquisite arrangement."[7]

Hume's work, one of the most enduring anti-Christian polemics ever, can do (along with the black-hole-space-alien crowd) nothing more than beg the question. Where did matter get the information and ability to organize itself into this "exquisite arrangement"? It's easier to imagine paper and ink, from something inherent in themselves, creating the manuscript for Dostoyevsky's *Crime and Punishment* than to conceive carbon, water, and proteins organizing themselves into a single cell, much less the processes that over time led to Einstein's brain.

MATTER AND ENERGY TEND DOWNWARD

This leads to another weakness in any theory of origins that denies God or any kind of a transcendent Creator greater and more powerful than the creation itself. One of the basic laws of physics is that things left to their own tend to wind down, diminish, or lose energy. Leave a cup of steaming tea in a place at room temperature and, over time, it doesn't get warmer or even stay warm. It loses energy.

Even with rain and sunshine, does your garden, without someone putting energy into it, get better or worse? Buildings, bodies, gardens—nothing left alone will evolve into something better, higher, or more organized and powerful. On the contrary, matter and energy tend downward, toward dissolution. Even an "open system" such as the earth (a system able to take in energy from sources outside it) will still wear out.

And yet we're supposed to believe that all the beauty, form, and complexity found in the creation arose solely from things less beautiful, less formed, and less complex. Or that atoms upgraded themselves to carbon and hydrogen and other elements and compounds that transformed themselves into flowers, trees, and beings capable of moral and ethical decisions.

"And do not forget," South African writer Laurens van der Post wrote, "it is a law of creation that that which is created can never be greater than the thing that created it."[8]

> It's more likely that a 100-pound woman in labor would give birth to a 150-pound baby than inanimate matter, in and of itself and regardless of how much time given it, would ever become even the "simplest" life form.

150-POUND BABY

How do inanimate materials—protons, electrons, molecules, atoms, even chemicals—emerge into something greater than their constituent parts (for example, life and human consciousness)? It's more likely that a 100-pound woman in labor would give birth to a 150-pound baby than inanimate matter, in and of itself and regardless of how much time given it, would ever become even the "simplest" life form, much less the vast variety of living things that we see all around us on earth.

If the needed elements weren't there to begin with—if they weren't in the original brew even in a potential form—then how did they arise from it? You can create interesting things with a handful of stones, but no matter how long or how creatively you shake them, crush them, or arrange them, they'll never become a living thing, because key elements needed for a living thing weren't in those stones to begin with. And time itself—far from creating those higher elements—would tend to wear down the stones, not transform them into something greater than they already were.

Leonardo da Vinci could draw his own self-portrait. His paintings could not draw themselves.

"By far," philosopher Étienne Gilson observed, "the hardest problem for philosophy and for science is to account for the existence of human wills in the world without ascribing to the first principle either a will or something which, because it virtually contains a will, is actually superior to it."[9]

Only something greater than a creation can make that creation. No one's surprised when an artist creates a self-portrait. What's impossible is for the self-portrait to create the artist. That would be going from something less intricate to something more intricate, and how can that be? Forces greater and smarter than a bicycle created the bicycle. It required something able to stand outside of it, to think of it, and then to amass the materials and processes needed to fashion it.

What, then, about the universe, and all that's in it? Only something greater than it could have created the universe—and who, or what, could that be but God, an eternal and all-powerful Creator deity like the one depicted in the Holy Scriptures? How much more reasonable to believe in such a Creator than in some of the alternatives that—with the exception of the concept of everything coming from *nothing*—don't even eliminate the need for a Creator anyway? And even *nothing*, it turns out, must be something after all, and where did that something, whatever it was, come from, if not from the Creator?

In short, if it's always wrong for anyone, anywhere, to believe anything upon insufficient evidence, then no wonder millions believe in God. Considering the evidence, how unreasonable not to?

WHO CREATED GOD?

And these millions believe not just in any deity, but in the God of the Holy Scriptures, the Creator God, the one in whom "we live and move and have our being" (Acts 17:28), the one "whose hand is the life of every living thing" (Job 12:10) and who has "created all things" (Revelation 4:11). How much more logical to believe in Him—as opposed to space aliens, black holes, or *nothing*—as the source of everything instead?

> Only two kinds of existence are possible: that which was created and that which has always existed and, thus, was never created. What other options are there?

But who created God?

British atheist Bertrand Russell told the story of how, in his youth, he wrestled with questions about the existence of God. Up until he was 18 years old, he said, he had believed in God, but then found himself confronted with the question of first causes. If everything that came into being had a cause—that something prior to it had created it—then what existed prior to God? *Who created God?* Russell had asked himself. From that point on, he said, he stopped believing that creation itself showed that God had to exist.

Yet the question "Who created God?" is misleading. It makes no sense because God, by definition, always existed (it's the same as asking, "Why is a circle round?").

Think about it. Only two kinds of existence are possible: that which was created (and once didn't exist) and that which has always existed and, thus, was never created. What other options are there? The God of the Bible falls into the latter category. That's why Scripture calls Him "the everlasting God" (Romans 16:26). However hard this concept is to grasp, what other logical conclusion can we draw?

SOMETHING ALWAYS CAUSES EVERYTHING

All around us we see things that are there only because something else caused them. Nothing comes from itself. Everything that once didn't exist but came into being (such as you, a house, a car, a zebra in your kitchen) did so because of something other than itself, something that was prior to it. Yet sooner or later we have to reach something that wasn't created, that did not result from something that existed before it, that instead was always there. And who, or what, could that be other than God? Anything else would need something to create it, and we're back where we started. Logically, then, something noncreated, something eternal, has to exist, and if that's not God, then what is it?

Nothing? Black holes? Space aliens?

Or an eternal self-existing God?

The New Testament declares about this God that "all things were made by him; *and without him was not any thing made that was made*" (John 1:4, KJV). In other words, anything that once did not exist

Tools do not create houses—intelligent people do.

but that came into being did so only through God, the deity depicted in the Holy Bible as the one who has always existed and through whom everything was created.

And He is God only because He is the Creator. "For by Him all things were created that are in heaven and that are on earth, visible and invisible, whether thrones or dominions or principalities or powers. All things were created through Him and for Him. And He is before all things, and in Him all things consist" (Colossians 1:16, 17).

The One who is before all things, the One who created all things, the One who holds all things together . . . no wonder He's God.

Who or what else would be?

In Our Beginning Is Our End

A spaceship from earth travels to a planet circling another star, one inhabited by beings much like humans. One major difference, however, is that—unlike humans—the inhabitants on this planet live for about 1 million years, give or take a few thousand. The astronauts from earth, as they mingle among these friendly inhabitants, soon notice something about them: they bemoan the meaningless and ultimate futility of their lives. "What can it all mean?" they wonder, particularly after a funeral. "We live what, 999,000 years, 1 million years, 1.1 million years—a speck, a flash in the face of eternity—and then what? Eternal death, eternal oblivion, eternal nothingness? What's the purpose of life if, in the end, we die forever and nothing comes after?"

Though imaginary, this little

> Our beginning, whether we wanted it or not, was in Christ, the Creator. And if we choose it, our end can be in Christ the Redeemer as well.

54

tale brings out an important point. Even if we accept the logical conclusion that God created us, we still ask, Why? What's our purpose? To spit out miserable generation after generation until, sooner or later, one of them blows itself up or freezes to death when the stars burn out and "the era of light is over"? If the question of God, and His existence, ended where it began, with Him as Creator, we're no better off than we would be as products of chance alone.

What kind of God put us here, gave us minds able to contemplate eternity and tremble before the temporality of our own existence, and then allows us all—without exception (or the possibility of exception)—to die? "Death's greasy thumbprint"[10] spoils everything human. It will make every heart as silent as a cut of raw beef, and will snap every neuron until a lifetime of memory disintegrates into the bellies of bacteria that will, themselves, disappear.

"Death's greasy thumbprint" spoils everything human.

REDEEMER

That's why, precisely, the God of the Bible isn't just our Creator. He did not just cage us in mortality like an animal in a zoo while the notion of immortality mocks us from beyond the bars. No—He's also the one who offers us eternal life, the only thing that can make our existence more than a farce. (Go to a graveyard sometime and eat a picnic lunch in the shadow of a tombstone. If what's in the ground below the picnic basket is your eternal destiny, how can it all not be a farce?)

Although God created us out of the ground (Genesis 2:7), He never intended to put us back there (God didn't create in order to kill). We were supposed to live off the soil, not become part of it.

That's why God is not just the Creator, He's the Redeemer—because without redemption nature itself, at least as it is now, works against us. We need, therefore, something that transcends nature, something stronger and above and outside of it—and that's God, our Redeemer God, whom Christians worship and know as Jesus Christ.

> We need something that transcends nature, something stronger and above and outside of it.

Why do Christians worship Jesus? Because He's not just Creator but also Redeemer. As such, He offers us hope beyond what this world can, which is the prospect of what? The big freeze, the big crunch, the big rip? Is that all we can hope for?

Scripture proclaims, "No! Hope for more, much more." And it shows us how, and through whom, and why we can hope for infinitely more.

"In my beginning," poet T. S. Eliot wrote, "is my end."[11] Our beginning, whether we wanted it or not, was in Christ, the Creator. And if we choose it, our end can be in Christ the Redeemer as well.

While we may have had no choice in our beginning, we do choose our end. And the hope of the Christian faith is that those who accept Christ, not just as their beginning (their Creator), but as their end (their Redeemer), have the promise of eternal redemption.

What is this redemption, however? What does it mean? Does it offer any kind of hope? And why do we believe in it?

That's what we'll look at next: redemption in Jesus—the essence of the Christian faith, the foundation of all its hope.

---

[1] http://members.aol.com/jeff1070/script.html; http://members.aol.com/jeff1070/wotw.html.

[2] In I. Barbour, *When Science Meets Religion*, p. 10.

[3] Michael J. Lemonick and J. Madeleine Nash, "Cosmic Conundrum," *Time*, Nov. 29, 2004, p. 58.

[4] Mark Steyn, "The Twentieth-Century Darwin," *Atlantic Monthly*, October 2004, p. 207.

[5] In Lemonick and Nash, p. 61.

[6] David Hume, *Dialogues Concerning Natural Religion* (London: Penguin

Books, 1990), p. 53.

[7] *Ibid.*, p. 56.

[8] Laurens van der Post, *A Walk With a White Bushman* (London: Chatto & Windus, 1986), p. 86.

[9] Étienne Gilson, *God and Philosophy* (New Haven, Conn.: Yale University Press, 1941), p. 22.

[10] Charles Simic, *Hotel Insomnia* (New York: Harcourt, Inc., 1992), p. 15.

[11] T. S. Eliot, "East Coker," *The Complete Poems and Plays* (New York: Harcourt Brace and Company, 1980), p. 123.

6

THE BOTTOM LINE

GOING IN CIRCLES

hat's harder to imagine: the universe as finite, or as infinite? If infinite, the universe just keeps going and going with no end, anywhere, ever. You travel at the speed of light for a billion years and get no closer to the edge than when you started . . . not the easiest concept to grasp (even with thousands of miles of neurons in our brains). But if finite, if the universe does have an end, that raises the question What's beyond the edge? Some argue that

Can we see beyond the edge of the universe?

58

The universe is expanding like a constantly inflating balloon.

the universe is finite but endless, like a circle on which one keeps going around and around, never stopping. Yet a circle's a circle because it is round, and something round demands space that it does not cover, just as something bounded demands a boundary with something else. So if the universe is bounded, what's beyond its border?

Meanwhile, whatever its size and shape, the universe keeps getting bigger and bigger too. Some ancients thought the universe extended not much farther beyond the earth, perhaps a few miles at most (ancient rabbinic tradition regarded God's throne as about three miles above the Temple in Jerusalem). A hundred years ago astronomers believed the universe to be about 5,000 light-years in diameter. Today astronomers estimate the visible part of the universe as about 27 billion light-years across, which means that if we scaled the universe down to the size of the earth's surface, our solar system would be the size of a small bacterium. Science claims that the universe is expanding, kind of like a balloon. And that's fine, but if the universe is, in fact, growing bigger, it leads to some mind-numbing questions, perhaps the most obvious being:

If the universe is expanding, what's it expanding into?

LITTLE THINGS

It's not just the macroworld—the big picture—that befuddles us, either. The other direction ties our brain cells into even worse knots.

Matter consists of atoms, entities so small that a drop of water contains billions of them. But the atom itself—a nucleus and the electron cloud around it—is cavernously empty. "Very roughly," the physicist John Gribbin wrote, "the proportion is like a grain of sand in Carnegie Hall. The empty hall is the 'atom'; the grain of sand is the 'nucleus.'"*

Meanwhile the nucleus contains protons and neutrons, themselves built from smaller components, called quarks. Some scientists theorize that quarks—all matter, actually—are made up of one-di-

"The proportion is like a grain of sand in Carnegie Hall. The empty hall is the 'atom'; the grain of sand is the 'nucleus.'"

mensional vibrating strings so small that a string is to the size of a proton as a proton is to the size of the solar system!

We're still not done. Matter, like numbers, is perhaps infinitely divisible. It just keeps getting smaller and smaller, with no smallest part, just as numbers can get smaller and smaller, with no smallest number.

THE BOTTOM LINE

In other words, existence, in both directions, might never end. Inward or outward, we're trapped, intellectually and physically, not only by the infinities around us but by the ones in us as well.

Creation—so great, so complex, so far beyond our thoughts—presents an awesome testimony to the power of the one who created it, the being through whom "all things were created that are in heaven and that are on earth, visible and invisible, whether thrones or dominions or principalities or powers. All things were created through Him and for Him. And He is before all things, and in Him all things consist" (Colossians 1:16, 17).

> We are so used to death that we regard it as the natural course of things, but death's a perversion of God's intended order.

But as we've already noted, this God is not only the Creator, He's also the Redeemer. He didn't put us here just to let us disappear forever into the infinities around us. No, He created us to have eternal life. Unfortunately, we are so used to death that we regard it as the natural course of things, just as a child raised in an abusive home assumes it's natural that parents beat their children. But death's a perversion of God's intended order, one to be removed. And that's what redemption is all about—the removal of death (as well as pain, sickness, and suffering). And it all happens through Jesus.

Scripture says: "Your attitude should be the same as that of Christ Jesus: Who, being in very nature God, did not consider equality with

God something to be grasped, but made himself nothing, taking the very nature of a servant, being made in human likeness. And being found in appearance as a man, he humbled himself and became obedient to death—even death on a cross!" (Philippians 2:5-8, NIV).

Put aside everything you assume about Christianity. Focus, instead, on this one point: At its core, Christianity teaches that the Creator of the universe, the power who made "all things" and through whom "all things consist," "made himself nothing, taking the very nature of a servant" and died on a cross. In other words, He purposely placed Himself under the judgment and punishment that the world (as we shall discover) itself deserved!

That's the bottom line.

Again, the existence of God, in and of itself, isn't necessarily good news. But what if this deity took upon Himself humanity, and in that humanity bore the punishment for all the evil that the human race has committed? What if He allowed Himself to be punished for all the bad things that we have done, because that was the only way we—as liars, cheaters, adulterers, slanderers, and even worse—could have the hope of eternal life?

Think of the implications.

NO CHEESY SENTIMENTALISM

> At its core, Christianity teaches that the Creator of the universe, the power who made "all things," made Himself nothing, and died on a cross. He purposely placed Himself under the judgment and punishment that the world itself deserved!

First, that the tingling of our skin when we sense that things will in the end turn out all right is based on reality, not on cheesy sentimentalism. That when we stare up at the night sky (whether it's muf-

fled in clouds or spangled with starlight), some- When we stare up
one's not only looking back but doing so with at the sky, someone
love and concern. That our lives are worth so looks back at us.
much more than this world could ever let on to.
That no matter how big the universe, the edges are closer than we
imagine. That something great awaits us, because otherwise why
would the Creator have gone through the sufferings He as a human
being did were not something wonderful to result? (Jesus didn't die
on the cross just to give sixteenth-century artists a subject to paint.)
And finally, that the greatest irony ever—our gravestones long out-
lasting us—will forever be reversed.

That, and so much more, is what it would mean.

With so much at stake, we ask, What is this redemption? Why do
we need it? How do we get it?

_____

* John Gribbin, *The Search for Superstrings, Symmetry, and the Theory of Everything* (New York: Little, Brown and Company, 1998), p. 6.

7

MORAL DILEMMA

LEFT OR RIGHT? RIGHT OR WRONG?

A 6-year-old girl from London went on her first trip to France. After collecting the luggage at the airport, the family hailed a cab curbside. The child, horrified, refused to get in.

"Mummy," she screamed, "they're driving on the wrong side of the road!"

Which is the "right" side?

That's like asking, Which is more beautiful, Beethoven's Ninth or Ozzy Osbourne's "Suicide Solution"? Some love Lucian

©PHOTODISC

Some cultures believe that touching a pig will defile.

Are morals as relative as preferring the music of Ludwig van Beethoven over that of Ozzy Osbourne?

Freud's art while others would question calling it "art" at all. Though many cultures cook most meals with pork, some believe that even touching a pig would defile them. Women obscenely obese in some societies are "supermodels" in others.

The point? In certain contexts, the issue isn't right and wrong, but culture, custom, and personal preference.

But what about morals? Are they as relative as one's preference for meaty thighs over skinny ones, or for Ozzy Osbourne over Beethoven? Some would argue, *Yes.* "There are no moral phenomena at all," German Friedrich Nietzsche trumpeted, "but only a moral interpretation of phenomena."[1] And though there's logic to that position, it does carry (as most positions do) some clumsy baggage.

A QUESTION OF TASTE

An atheist and a Christian began debating morality, the Christian arguing that moral values came from God, the atheist that they were

Is trying to break free from Islamic dress styles a crime?

purely human creations, arising from personal feelings and nothing more. As such, the atheist continued, no one could justifiably claim one moral as superior to another. "Kind sir," the Christian replied, "in some societies people love their neighbors while in others they eat them, all based on moral codes. Which do you prefer?"

A few years ago a young Turkish woman, the mother of a 5-year-old, was shot dead at a bus stop in Berlin, one of a half dozen Turkish women murdered in "honor killings" by close relatives.

"In the past four months," a German publication reported, "six Muslim women living in Berlin have been brutally murdered by family members. Their crime? Trying to break free and live Western lifestyles. Within their communities, the killers are revered as heroes for preserving their family dignity. How can such a horrific and shockingly archaic practice be flourishing in the heart of Europe?"[2]

"Horrific and shockingly archaic practice"? How judgmental! If morals are, like art and music, human creations alone, who has the right to judge something another culture believes is moral, even honorable? Is not the outrage the Germans felt a moral *interpretation* of the events, nothing more? Since morality is created only by humans, the calling of "honor killings" or cannibalism wrong is like labeling a preference for the rumba over the tango "wrong."

MORAL DILEMMA

Yet we sense that certain things are not right, regardless of whatever the cultural, traditional, and preferential claims used to defend them. We're no more justified in deeming certain actions morally relative than we are in equating the desire to exterminate one group of people and not another with the desire to eat one kind of food and not another.

Why do we conclude this? Again, if morality is horizontal, arising from within humanity, as opposed to being placed upon it from something outside of it, such as God, then what grounds does anyone have for condemning murder, torture, theft, incest, and so forth if such things are, in a particular culture, accepted as moral, legal, and perhaps even honorable?

Suppose a nation claimed that for its own good it must kill all 3-year-olds with red hair, and that a supermajority of the populace agreed with the law to the point that they even wrote it in their constitution. Most of us reading this would still argue that it wasn't right. But if we are convinced that it's still not right, regardless of how many people (even the whole world) agreed with it, then there must be a morality that transcends culture, law, and tradition, one that exists in a realm beyond the human. And where could such a concept of right and wrong come from, other than God? It certainly didn't emerge from a chance confluence of molecules and chemicals, did it?

Again, if we remember Clifford's principle ("It is always wrong, everywhere, and for anyone, to believe anything upon insufficient evidence"), then to assume that morality accidentally arose from chemicals would seem

> "In some societies people love their neighbors while in others they eat them, all based on moral codes."

to violate the principle, would it not? After all, what evidence do we have that inanimate chemicals (carbon, hydrogen, oxygen, nitrogen) could, in and of themselves, ever produce a transcendent morality?

If we concede a morality that goes beyond culture and custom, one that isn't a human concoction any more than the laws that govern planetary movements, then other questions arise, such as: (1) What is this morality code? and (2) What are the consequences of violating it?

---

[1] Friedrich Nietzsche, *Beyond Good and Evil* (New York: Random House, 1996), p. 85.

[2] Spiegel Online, Mar. 2, 2005 (http://service.spiegel.de/cache/international/0,1518,344374,00.html).

8

TYPHOID MARY

WHAT DO WE LIVE FOR?

oet James Tate wrote about an office employee musing about what a hustler the new manager, Preston Cooper, was. The narrator thought to himself how his boss pretended to be very low-key, when in fact his ambition obsessed him. One day the manager popped his head into the employee's office and gave him a pep talk about how well he, the worker, was doing, with sales growing in markets all over the country. The manager then announced, "I smell a big bonus coming,

Scientists talk about the butterfly effect, the idea that even the most insignificant events, such as a butterfly flapping its wings, can have monstrous effects later, triggering storms and other events that can change lives. Just look at Typhoid Mary.

Mortie. Keep pushing, and don't give an inch. Bomb 'em back into the Stone Age," he declared before disappearing with a laugh.

Mortie continues to think about Preston Cooper and what it was like working under him in the office. Ever since Preston had arrived it was as if the office had gone to war. The narrator had mixed feelings about the new attitude. While sometimes it was fun, at other times he was not sure. After all, they were not protecting their country from some enemy; they were just selling potato chips.[1]

THE DIALS OF THE UNIVERSE

Potato chips? Is it moral to be so ferocious, so fanatical, so devoted to something as the sale of potato chips?

It depends upon where morality comes from, how it's formed, and how strictly we must adhere to it. Interestingly, we can learn something about morality from (*of all things*) physics!

As we have already noted, during the past few decades scientists

©PHOTODISC

Cover the entire North American continent in dimes all the way up to the moon.

have been surprised at just how suitable for human life the cosmos is. One could be excused, almost, for thinking that the universe had been made exclusively just for us. It's as if the universe is maintained by numerous dials so precariously balanced that the slightest misadjustment of even one of them would prevent human life as we know it from existing. God's physical laws, it seems, allow for little violation.

For example: "Unless the number of electrons is equivalent to the number of protons to an accuracy of one part in 10^{37}, or better, electromagnetic forces in the universe would have so overcome gravitational forces that galaxies, stars, and planets never would have formed.

"One part in 10^{37} is such an incredibly sensitive balance that it is hard to visualize. The following analogy might help: Cover the entire North American continent in dimes all the way up to the moon, a height of about 239,000 miles. . . . Next, pile dimes from here to the moon on a billion other continents the same size as North America. Paint one dime red and mix it into the billion piles of dimes. Blindfold a friend and ask him to pick out one dime. The odds that he will pick the red dime are one in 10^{37}. And this is only one of the parameters that is so delicately balanced to allow life to form."[2]

Other delicate balances exist as well, with variables even more unforgiving than the one above (ratios such as $1:10^{40}$ or $1:10^{60}$)—relationships that demand a precision far beyond what most human-made science would dare dream of achieving.

MORAL DIALS

However much these incredible balances indicate design (hence a Designer), they could suggest something else, too. As we've seen, we're submerged (apparently) in a transcendent morality, one not of human origin, but from above—otherwise it wouldn't be wrong to murder all children with red hair if everyone agreed that it was permissible. Because we sense that it would still be wrong no matter how many approved of it, such morality must arise from something other than us. And because it's unlikely, if not impossible, that this morality emerged from mere chemical processes (accidental ones at that), the most obvious other source would be God, a deity who, as He created the universe with physical laws, also endowed it with moral ones. If so, and these moral laws do exist, what parallels might exist between them and what we see in nature?

> Suppose that God's moral laws were just as precise, just as finely tuned, as His physical ones. It's one thing to have a physical law precise to $1:10^{60}$. But could you imagine a moral law with a margin of error just as refined?

"The orders of nature," theologian Paul Tillich stated, "are analogous to the order of the moral law."[3]

Analogous? In what ways?

Suppose, for instance, that God's moral laws were just as precise, just as finely tuned, as His physical ones. Consider that such transcendent morality was just as unyielding, just as intolerant of deviation or violation, as the physical constants mentioned above. It's one thing to have a physical law precise to $1:10^{60}$. But could you imagine a moral law with a margin of error just as refined?

Scripture does teach what we do sense: that there exists a transcendent moral law that overrules all human ones. It's commonly known as the Ten Commandments, and though dramatically revealed to a specific people at a specific time (the Israelite nation at Mount Sinai), it was in effect long before the powerful expression of it at Sinai, and it's still valid today.

GOD'S MORAL LAW

Think about it. Has there ever been a time or a place on earth that injunctions against such things as murder, adultery, theft, lying, and so forth weren't in effect? If the Ten Commandments compose the revealed principles of God's morality for us—one that supersedes any human law, custom, or tradition (after all, if God declares adultery wrong, then it's not acceptable no matter how many human laws or traditions say it's right)—then it's hard to imagine that they weren't always valid, at least whenever there were human beings. Think of the physical chaos that would ensue were God to suspend His physical laws. Is there any reason, then, to suppose that He abrogate His moral ones as well, which would mean that as far as God was concerned, murder, stealing, lying, and so forth were OK in any and all circumstances?

> Has there ever been a time or a place on earth that injunctions against such things as murder, adultery, theft, lying, and so forth weren't in effect?

If the Ten Commandments comprise this moral law, how much deviation is allowed? If God's moral laws parallel some of the physical ones, then the amount of wiggle room would be, it would seem, almost nonexistent.

For example, almost everyone has heard of the commandment "You shall not murder" (Exodus 20:13). It sounds reasonable enough, all things considered. But how closely is it to be followed?

Jesus said: "You have heard that it was said to those of old, 'You shall not murder, and whoever murders will be in danger of the judgment.' But I say to you that whoever is angry with his brother without a cause shall be in danger of the judgment" (Matthew 5:21, 22).

The same with the commandment about adultery. Jesus said: "You have heard that it was said to those of old, 'You shall not commit adultery.' But I say to you that whoever looks at a woman to lust for her has already committed adultery with her in his heart" (verses 27, 28).

Though we can't directly compare an adultery:lust-in-the-heart ratio to a $1:10^{60}$ ratio, the principle is there: God's moral law doesn't allow for violation any more than His physical ones do.

Where does this leave us, beings known to steal everything from our neighbor's water bucket to our neighbor's spouse, beings who, wrote Frenchman Jean-Jacques Rousseau, can live together only by "obstructing, supplanting, deceiving, betraying, destroying one another"?[4]

It would leave us condemned, right? No doubt about it.

And that's why—precisely why—we need redemption.

TYPHOID MARY

In 1906 a wealthy New York banker named Charles Henry Warren rented a vacation home for a few weeks in the Long Island town of Oyster Bay, New York. Within a few weeks some of his daughters became ill with the dreaded typhoid fever. Before long, the maids, his wife, and the gardener came down with the disease too. Half the house got sick. At first they thought it was the water, but further investigation showed that their cook, a young Irish immigrant girl named Mary Mallon (who had left a few weeks after the outbreak) was the carrier.

Typhoid Mary in a 1909 newspaper illustration.

An investigator discovered that typhoid outbreaks had followed Mary wherever she worked, even though she herself was, apparently, healthy. Mary cooked in a house in Mamaroneck, New York, for about two weeks before its residents contracted typhoid. She then took a position in a large home in Manhattan in 1901, where its inhabitants soon caught the disease (their launderer died from it). Next, she went to cook for a lawyer, and seven of eight members of the household developed typhoid (what's most ironic is that Mary spent months helping to care for the people she unwittingly made sick).

Mary Mallon (left) in a hospital bed during her first quarantine.

Convinced that the young immigrant was the source, the investigator, George Soper, found Mary working at another house and approached her, albeit cautiously. (How would you react, having a total stranger come up to you and accuse you of carrying a deadly bacterium, even though you felt perfectly fine, and then ask you for stool, blood, and urine samples?)

"I had my first talk with Mary in the kitchen of this house. . . . I was as diplomatic as possible, but I had to say that I suspected her of making people sick and that I wanted specimens of her urine, feces, and blood. It did not take Mary long to react to this suggestion. She seized a carving fork and advanced in my direction. I passed rapidly down the long narrow hall, through the tall iron gate, . . . and so to the sidewalk. I felt rather lucky to escape."[5]

As other health officials approached her, she refused to cooperate, arguing that since she was healthy, she could not possibly be carrying a deadly disease. After Mary refused all attempts to submit voluntarily, health officials took her by force to a hospital, where tests confirmed that she was a "healthy carrier" of typhoid, meaning that although she was infected with the disease, she had no symptoms.

The authorities kept the young woman isolated in a hospital on North Brother Island near the Bronx, even though there were no laws that allowed the government to incarcerate someone who had not been charged with a crime. Mary, for her part, continued to insist that she was not the carrier (after all, she wasn't sick!), and that the authorities were persecuting her because she was Irish and an immigrant. She sued the health department, contending that her imprisonment was illegal.

"I have committed no crime," she said, "and I am treated like an outcast—a criminal. It is unjust, outrageous, uncivilized. It seems incredible that in a Christian community a defenseless woman can be treated in this manner."[6]

A judge, however, ruled against her, and she spent three years on the island. Then a new health commissioner released her on the condition that she not work with food. After trying other odd jobs, Mary changed her name to Mrs. Brown and obtained a job cooking at a hospital in Manhattan. Before long, 25 people came down with the disease, two of whom died. Quickly caught, she ended up quarantined on the same island for the next 23 years, where she died of pneumonia in 1938. An autopsy revealed that she was still actively carrying typhoid.

One person, very negative effects.

Compare that to the taint and effects of sin, multiply that by the billions of human beings who have ever lived, and you will start to understand the problem that the human race faces.

BUTTERFLY EFFECT

In his novel *Infinite Jest* David Foster Wallace tells about a teenage tennis player who kills himself by drinking cyanide in a glass of Nestlé's Quik. The father, hearing "the thump of the kid keeling over," rushes into

© ISTOCKPHOTO.COM/REDMAL

the kitchen and administers mouth-to-mouth resuscitation. Only problem is that pop gets some of the "NaCN-laced Quik in his mouth" and dies. Mom enters and "sees them both lying there bright blue and stiffening" and she gives the dad mouth-to-mouth, only to drop dead too. This unfortunate family has six more kids, all trained in mouth-to-mouth, and so "by the end of the night the whole family's lying there blue-hued and stiff as posts."[7]

> **None of us live in a vacuum. Our lives and actions influence others, exponentially.**

However far-fetched and silly the story might seem at first glance, it presents a truth that's neither—none of us live in a vacuum. Our lives and actions influence others, exponentially and often negatively, too. Just look at Typhoid Mary. Scientists talk about the butterfly effect, the idea that even the most insignificant events, such as a butterfly flapping its wings, can have monstrous effects later, triggering storms and other events that can change lives.

What happens when we humans violate, in a big way, God's moral law? The Bible has a term, one that we have repeatedly used in this book: "Everyone who sins breaks the law; in fact, sin is lawlessness" (1 John 3:4, NIV). And according to the Bible, such violation of God's law has led all humanity down the path to calamity and ruin. After all, if disregarding God's physical laws would have meant that human life couldn't have even started, what would ignoring His moral laws do to that same human life after it had? Scripture tells us: "Therefore, just as sin entered the world through one man, and death through sin, and in this way death came to all men, because all sinned" (Romans 5:12, NIV). Breaking God's physical laws would have stopped us from existing. Violating the moral ones achieves the same goal, only more slowly.

"The wages of sin," Scripture says, "is death" (Romans 6:23). While death itself is bad enough, the path to it always comes lined with pain, sickness, loss, alienation, and fear, hecklers that mock us every step. And no matter how ferociously and passionately we jeer back, death always wins, so what's the point of the whole walk to begin with?

THE MOST URGENT OF QUESTIONS

British author and atheist Bryan Magee wrote that because of the looming reality of death, whatever he did (or didn't do) in his life, "none of it would make the slightest difference to me or to anyone else when all of us were nothing, as everyone was going to be, including everyone not yet born: that it could therefore make no difference *when* I died, and would have made no difference if I had never been born; that I was in any event going to be for all eternity what I would have been if I had never been born; that there was no meaning to any of it, no point in any of it; and that in the end everything was nothing."[8]

If, as Frenchman Albert Camus claimed, "the meaning of life is the most urgent of questions,"[9] then until we answer the question of death we can't resolve the question of life, because (as Bryan Magee understood) death denudes life of not just breath, or sentience, but of meaning, too. Sure, after thousands of years of progress, we might be able to hold off death a little longer than in the days that physicians used cow dung in medicinal elixirs or leeches to treat disease, but all our attempts to solve

"The meaning of life is the most urgent of questions," Albert Camus claimed.

> **Unless something solves the problem of sin, that of death never will be.**

the problem of death have been about as effective as blotting out with a crayon the fat content on a box of doughnuts in order to solve the problem of obesity.

Death began with one thing: sin—the violation of God's moral law. Unless something solves the problem of sin, that of death never will be. And that's what the whole plan of redemption is about: God Himself dealing with the problem of sin, hence the dilemma of death. Sure, we all still die, but because of the work of redemption by Jesus, our death is a temporary rest only, a sleep, and not our eternal destiny, as it would otherwise be.

"I TELL YOU A MYSTERY"

"Behold, I tell you a mystery: We shall not all sleep, but we shall all be changed—in a moment, in the twinkling of an eye, at the last trumpet. For the trumpet will sound, and the dead will be raised incorruptible, and we shall be changed. For this corruptible must put on incorruption, and this mortal must put on immortality. So when this corruptible has put on incorruption, and this mortal has put on immortality, then shall be brought to pass the saying that is written, 'Death is swallowed up in victory.' 'O death, where is your sting? O Hades, where is your victory?'" (1 Corinthians 15:51-55).

"And God will wipe away every tear from their eyes; there shall be no more death, nor sorrow, nor crying. There shall be no more pain, for the former things have passed away" (Revelation 21:4).

All our attempts to end death fail because they deal with it only on the physical level (where else could we go, actually?), and yet the physical is only the symptom of the problem, not the cause. The cause, as we said, is sin (violation of God's law), which is why the answer has to be found at that level (the level of sin) as well.

Hence, enter Jesus Christ.

[1] James Tate, *Return to the City of White Donkeys* (New York: HarperCollins, 2004), p. 41.

[2] Hugh Ross, *The Creator and the Cosmos* (Colorado Springs, Colo.: NavPress Publishing Group, 1995), p. 115.

[3] Paul Tillich, *Biblical Religion and the Search for Ultimate Reality* (Chicago: University of Chicago Press, 1955), p. 40.

[4] Jean-Jacques Rousseau, *The* Discourses *and Other Early Political Writings* (Cambridge, Mass.: Cambridge University Press, 1997), p. 100.

[5] http://history1900s.about.com/od/1900s/a/typhoidmary.htm.

[6] *Ibid.*

[7] David Foster Wallace, *Infinite Jest* (New York: Little, Brown and Company, 1996), pp. 436, 437.

[8] Bryan Magee, *Confessions of a Philosopher* (New York: Random House, 1997), p. 252.

[9] Albert Camus, *The Myth of Sisyphus and Other Essays* (New York: Random House, 1955), p. 4.

THE HENRY VIII FACTOR

LA GUARDIA AND THE LAW

iorello Enrico La Guardia was a judge during the hard years of the Depression, a time—rare in America—when people didn't always have enough food. One day the police brought a father into his courtroom. The charge? Having stolen some bread. When asked by Judge La Guardia why he did it, the man, sobbing, said it was to feed his hungry children. La Guardia asked him if he understood that he had committed a crime. The man, penitent, barely raising his eyes, nodded and said, "Yes, sir."

Judge Fiorello Enrico La Guardia

Sternly La Guardia then said that he had to punish him, because "the law makes no exceptions."

The man again nodded.

Judge La Guardia then put his hand into his pocket, took out $10, and said, "Here's the payment for your fine. I pay it myself. Though guilty, you will not face the penalty yourself."

What Judge La Guardia did for the man is what Jesus did for every human being, only the guilt of sin didn't require $10, $1,000, or $1 million. It demanded the life of the offender. Sin is a capital offense, because the sinner is a misfit in a perfectly moral universe. And though one can be impressed with the generosity and kindness of La Guardia, one wonders what he would have done had the law demanded, not $10, but death! How readily would the judge have paid the offender's offense then?

Yet that is exactly what Jesus did for us. He paid the penalty for the sins that we have committed, and that penalty was death. Here is the plan of redemption, pure and simple—Jesus suffered the penalty of sin, in our behalf, so that none of us ever have to. And He was able to do it because He did for us what we can't—obey the moral law of the universe with the kind of perfection it demands. That's why the Bible says: "Therefore by the deeds of the law no flesh will be justified in His sight" (Romans 3:20). "For we maintain that a man is justified by faith apart from observing the law" (verse 28, NIV). "A man is not justified by observing the law, but by faith in Jesus Christ" (Galatians 2:16, NIV). "Clearly no one is justified before God by the law" (Galatians 3:11, NIV).

THE MIRROR PRINCIPLE

But why not? Why can't we be justified by the law?

Well . . . for starters, the law wasn't made to justify us. It, in fact, condemns us, for "by the law is the knowledge of sin" (Romans 3:20). The law is to sin as an X-ray is to a broken bone. The X-ray (law), far from healing the broken bone (sin), simply points it out.

©PHOTODISC

The mirror shows us what we look like— it cannot change us.

Imagine burning and scarring your face. You can't view the scars unless you look in the mirror. Yet looking the mirror, no matter how often, doesn't cause the scar to go away. It only makes you see it more and more. The mirror shows you just how bad you really look. That's what the law is: the mirror that reveals to us our sins. Indeed, it throws them back in our face.

Now comes redemption. Like the judge, God didn't throw away His moral law or lower its standard. Just as no one can nullify the consequences of violating physical laws, neither can we stop the consequences of breaking moral ones. Instead, through the life and ministry of Jesus (the only one in human flesh who ever kept the law perfectly), through His life and ministry, made a way to meet its demands. Jesus never violated the law, not even to a $1:10^{37}$ ratio, and the essence of the Christian faith is that God will credit Christ's flawless record to us.

"Since we are sinful, unholy, we cannot perfectly obey the holy law. We have no righteousness of our own with which to meet the claims of the law of God. But Christ has made a way of escape for us. He lived on earth amid trials and temptations such as we have to meet. He lived a sinless life. He died for us, and now He offers to take our sins and give us His righteousness. If you give yourself to Him, and accept Him as your Savior, then, sinful as your life may have been, for His sake you are accounted righteous. Christ's character stands in place of your character, and you are accepted before God just as if you had not sinned."[1]

> Just as no one can nullify the consequences of violating physical laws, neither can we stop the consequences of breaking moral ones.

Scripture depicts Jesus as sinless, as having never once broken God's law. "For He made Him who knew no sin to be sin for us, that we might become the righteousness of God in Him" (2 Corinthians 5:21). "And you know that He was manifested to take away our sins, and in Him there is no sin" (1 John 3:5). The Bible says that Jesus "was in all points tempted as we are, yet without sin" (Hebrews 4:15). Jesus accomplished what no one else ever has, which is to live a life of perfect holiness, perfect righteousness. He had what Scripture calls "the righteousness of God" (Romans 3:22), that is, a righteousness equal to that of God Himself, which isn't surprising, because Jesus was Himself God except that, for the years of His ministry on earth, He covered His deity in humanity (our humanity), and in that humanity lived as one of us, only without succumbing to any of the temptations that we easily immerse ourselves in with unbridled passion.

No Longer Held Against Us

The great provision of the gospel, the essence of the message that Christians have, is that our past deeds—even the ones that we have no excuse for other than our own seething self-gratification, no justification for other than our own hateful lusts and desires—will no longer be held against us, because, if we claim it for ourselves, the perfect life of Jesus will be ours. His righteousness, the righteousness of God Himself, will be considered our righteousness, and so all the things that we have done, even the ones that curdle our soul in guilt, will be in a sense wiped clean before God, and we'll have a new beginning with Him. Whereas we, time and again, have allowed temptation to dominate us, Jesus never once gave in—and the great news is that His record of successes can before God be accounted as ours.

That's the hope that Jesus offers the world. Seeking to work our way back to God through good deeds is about as useless as multiplying any number—20, or 50, or 10,000, or 16 million—by 0 in an attempt to reach 1. It's an impossible endeavor. That's why Jesus came, assumed our flesh, and lived a perfect life—so that His life can be credited to us as if it were our own. Without that substitution, we would stand condemned by God's moral law, the cosmic law that defines right and wrong, good and evil above and beyond all human laws, customs, and traditions, and that allows for no more deviation than does the physical law that governs the ratio between the number of electrons and protons.

> Seeking to work our way back to God through good deeds is about as useless as multiplying any number by 0 in an attempt to reach 1.

WHERE'S THE JUSTICE?

If Christ's perfect record can cover our sins, and we stand before God in a moral perfection that we didn't earn, in a status that we didn't deserve, what about justice? How just or fair is it that violators of God's moral law should escape the punishment that the divine law demands? What good is such law if even the most egregious transgressors receive clemency? And what about the havoc resulting from their sin? Every death, every sickness, every war, every pain of every human being originates from violation of God's law, not necessarily on an individual level (as if each person's sufferings were the direct result of his or her own sins), but corporately—like those whose homes get flooded in a hurricane triggered by global warming, or whose lives have been ruined by wars that they didn't start.

"If we could lay all the world's misery," wrote German philosopher

©PHOTODISIC

Humanity can suffer from the consequences of corporate actions, as during flooding caused by the results of human-induced globabl warming.

©PHOTODISC

Arthur Schopenhauer, "in one pan of the weighing-scales, and all the world's guilt in the other, the point would certainly indicate that they [were] equally heavy."[2]

Guilt and misery equally heavy? The guilt must be immeasurable (the misery certainly is). *And yet, through Jesus, that guilt can be pardoned, fully and completely?* How so? Doesn't the law demand punishment, and justice restitution? What happens to guilt, to punishment, to fairness, if Jesus' perfect life becomes credited even to scoundrels? That's mercy, but where's the justice?

We find it in the death of Jesus, that's where. As God Himself, Jesus made everything—not just the physical laws that govern the universe, but the moral laws, too. As the one who established moral law, He stands equal to (even above) it—just as an artist who makes a creation stands equal to (or even above) it as well. Therefore, as the only one in that role, that of being greater than the law, Jesus alone could satisfy its demands.

But what does this mean?

DEBTOR'S PRISON

Imagine being hopelessly in debt to the point that even if all your friends pooled their wealth, they couldn't touch the interest, much less the principal. Suppose, too, a friend announced, out of nowhere, that on his own authority the debt is canceled. His pronouncement, of course, could no more cancel your debt than the Russian Duma decreeing that the next full moon should remain in the sky forever to provide endless bright nights on the Siberian tundra.

Who alone can cancel the debt? Of course, only the one to which payment is owed.

But there still remains that nagging question about justice. Is it fair to cancel a debt? Suppose you signed a contract saying that if you owed money, *you'd* pay it back, or that *you'd* make sure it got dealt with one way or another. Perhaps the contract was so sacred that it could not be violated without a gross injustice being done. The debt, therefore, can't be canceled. It has to be paid. And suppose, too, that the only one who has the money to pay the debt happens to be the one to whom it's owed.

There's only one option, then, for justice and payment. Instead of canceling the debt, the one *owed* the money pays it! Wanting to free you from an impossible debt, and yet unable to cancel it (at least without being unjust), he takes care of it himself. Justice is done because the debt's not canceled, and yet you're free from that debt through the generosity of the one who assumed it for you.

Now, according to the Bible, we've all violated God's law, and so we all owe a debt to Him, one that we can't pay, at least not without forfeiting eternal life. Only God can cancel that debt, because only to Him is it owed. But since His justice doesn't allow Him to cancel the debt, He—God—pays it Himself!

God wants to free you from the debt you owe Him.

Here's essentially the concept behind Jesus' death on the cross, the reason that He died. His death met justice, for the debt had been paid, but paid by the only one who could satisfy the demands of the law. Not only had He kept it perfectly; He had created it to begin with. "The substitute for the law-breakers," wrote British theologian John Stott, "is none other than the Lawmaker himself."[3]

Jesus died in order that God "might be just, and the justifier of him which believeth in Jesus" (Romans 3:26, KJV). The Lord showed justice in that He didn't violate a basic truth, which is that sin leads to death. "The wages of sin is death" (Romans 6:23). And yet He showed His mercy, because, by taking the punishment that we deserve, He freed us from the penalty of our sins. We don't have to face the final judgment against our sins, because Jesus faced that judgment for us at the cross.

"A FAR, FAR BETTER THING . . ."

Charles Dickens set his *Tale of Two Cities* against the background of the French Revolution, or at least the phase known as the Reign of Terror, in which state-inspired mob violence got so bad, with so many people getting guillotined, that the smell of blood, which literally flowed through the streets of Paris, caused a drop in the real estate market in the neighborhoods in which the executions took place.

In Dickens' tale, among those condemned is a young father named Charles Darnay, whose capital offense is that he belongs to an aristocratic family, a death sentence for many during the Reign of Terror.

But then comes Sydney Carton, who in Dickens' story is a lazy alcoholic lawyer totally detached and uninterested in anything about anyone, including himself. The character acknowledges that his life is pretty much a waste (it reminds one of Albert Camus' famous existentialist deadbeat Meursault in *The Stranger*). However, by the story's

©MICHAEL

Dickens' *Tale of Two Cities* tells of redemption when the guillotine reigned in Paris.

One man perished for the whole world.

end, Sydney manages to switch places with Charles, so that the young aristocrat can escape and he, Sydney, can die in his stead.

Amid the mob hysteria, the switch goes undetected. As the rabble carries Sydney down the street, they believe that it is Charles. When they hurl insults, they assume that it is Charles they are insulting. As they place his head in the guillotine, they consider it Charles's head. And when the blade falls and takes his life, they believe that it is Charles's life they have ended.

It is a far, far better thing that I do, than I have ever done, Sydney thinks just before the blade drops. *It is a far, far better rest that I go to than I have ever known.*[4]

In Dickens' novel one man died in place of one man. But through Jesus, one man perished for the whole world—for every person, regardless of who they are, where they live, or what their sins have been. Yet Christ's death doesn't automatically give every person eternal life. Why not?

It's simple. We have to ask for it.

MERELY FOR THE ASKING

Yes, the great news of Christianity is that we can have the provision made for us merely by asking for it. Yes, by *asking* for it.

If you think about it, how else could it be? We can't earn it, not with the demands of the law being beyond what we could ever meet. Instead, we claim that righteousness, not because we deserve it

> The great news of Christianity is that we can have the provision made for us merely by asking for it.

(we don't), but because it's our only hope. Without it we have nothing. Our great need is our only claim to it, and we can take it because

> **Christ's death is real, and our belief doesn't change that fact any more than not believing the earth is round makes it not round. What our belief alters is the application of His death in our lives.**

God has offered it to us. Christianity calls God's gift of salvation to us "grace." This righteousness, this perfection, this salvation, becomes ours, not by our efforts or obedience, but *by faith.* That is, we believe it and then we claim it for ourselves. If we can't earn it, then we have to accept it through trust in God's power to accomplish what He promises.

Salvation is one of the few things in reality that becomes true *only* because we believe it's true. Yes, Christ's death is real, regardless of whether we acknowledge it or not. Our belief doesn't change that fact any more than not believing the earth is round makes it not round. What our belief does alter is *the application* of His death in our lives. When we believe and accept it, that belief and acceptance makes salvation valid for us personally.

Christians call this justification *by faith.* "Therefore we conclude that a man is justified by faith apart from the deeds of the law" (Romans 3:28). Jesus died for our sins in order that we can have eternal life, but this eternal life doesn't automatically bestow itself on everyone. Only those who claim it by faith will actually receive it.

This great news of justification by faith is the essence of Christianity's message to the world. Everything else is, indeed, commentary.

The existence of God, in and of itself, isn't necessarily good news. But what if this God took upon Himself humanity, and in that humanity bore the punishment for all the evil that humanity has committed? What if He allowed Himself to be punished for all the bad things we have done? And what if He took this punishment upon

Himself because that was the only way we—as liars, cheaters, adulterers, slanderers, even worse—could have the hope of eternal life? And what if that hope is offered to us by this God only by faith—absolute trust in it?

That's the God of the Bible, the deity revealed in Jesus Christ, who said, "He who has seen Me has seen the Father" (John 14:9).

No wonder, then, that so many love, literally, what they discover in this biblical teaching.

THE HENRY THE VIII FACTOR

Even the sleaziest and most far-fetched Hollywood scriptwriter couldn't compete with the story of Henry VIII (1491-1547) and his six wives, all of whom met various fates: Catherine of Aragon (divorced); Ann Boleyn (executed); Jane Seymour (died in childbirth); Anne of Cleves (divorced); Kathryn Howard (executed); Catherine Parr (widowed).

Why did he have so many wives?

Henry produced six kids with Catherine of Aragon; all but one, a girl, died. With Catherine's supply of fertile eggs fast depleting, Henry, if he wanted to fulfill his dynastic ambitions (i.e., produce a male heir), would have to find another womb, which he did: Anne Boleyn's. Anne, however, wouldn't share Henry's bed unless he shared his throne, which meant divorcing Catherine. The law, however, wouldn't allow it.

So what did Henry VIII do? Rewrite the law, what else? He overturned the ecclesiastical and political legal landscape in order to make the law meet him where he was at. "Henry and Parliament finally threw off England's allegiance to Rome in an un-

PUBLIC DOMAIN

King Henry VIII sought to solve his problem by changing the law of the land.

Anne Boleyn wouldn't share Henry's bed unless he shared his throne.

surpassed burst of revolutionary statute-making: the Act of Annates (1532), the Act of Appeals (1533), the Act of Supremacy (1534), the First Act of Succession (1534), the Treasons Act (1534), and the Act Against the Pope's Authority (1536)."[5] The English king didn't change himself or his actions in order to meet the demands of the law. No, he altered the requirements of the law in order to meet his own actions. Nothing was so sacred about the laws that they couldn't be changed.

That was a real kingdom. Let's consider an imaginary one that we'll call Antinomia. The king of Antinomia has a son, a hopeless reprobate who vandalizes a famous statue in the capital. The law demands the strict punishment of five years in jail, no exceptions, for his crime. What does the king do? Well, he changes the law so that it's no longer a criminal act to vandalize the statue. That way his son, who should have been punished, isn't, because what he did is no longer a crime.

Now imagine the same scenario but with only one difference. Suppose the law were so sacred that the king himself won't change it. He could but doesn't. Although the law demands punishment, the ruler loves his son so much that he doesn't want him to face the penalty. What does the king do? He takes the punishment himself, substituting himself for the son so that (1) the demands of the law get met and justice done, and (2) he spares his son the pain of the judgment.

This story (the second version) is analogous to the biblical gospel, the self-substitution of God in our place. Jesus paid for our violation of the law, fulfilling its demands while we, as breakers of that law, do not get punished.

Scripture, as we saw, said that "sin is lawlessness," or as the King James Version puts it, "sin is the transgression of the law" (1 John 3:4), and all sin leads to death. The gospel teaches, however, that

Jesus faced that death for us so that we wouldn't have to experience it ourselves. In other words, He endured the penalty for *our* violation of God's law.

THE COST OF THE CROSS

What, then, does the death of Jesus say about the law of God (the Ten Commandments), that its demands *had to be* answered? Wouldn't it have been so much easier if God had done what Henry VIII or the ruler of Antinomia (first version) did—change the law to meet transgressors where they were, in their violation of His law? When you think about the cost of the cross—God bearing in Himself the sins and the suffering and the guilt of all humanity—wouldn't it have been less costly just to have "lowered the bar," to have modified divine law in order that acts once deemed violations no longer were? If it's against the law to walk on the grass, yet everyone does, why not just get rid of the law forbidding it? How much easier for God Himself to have changed the definition of sin to meet humanity's present condition rather than to bear, in Himself, the penalty for humanity's sin.

Poet Bertolt Brecht wrote "The Democratic Judge," which tells the following story of an Italian restaurant owner who sought American citizenship and appeared before the judge in charge of examining those seeking it. Because of his ignorance of the E nglish language, the immigrant kept responding to the judge's questions with "1492," the date of Columbus's discovery of the New World. The official had no choice but to deny the man's application and send him home. The would-be citizen did not give up, even though his struggles to learn the language proved fruitless. Each time he would always answer each question

Statue of Brecht outside the Berliner Ensemble's theater in Berlin

GNU FREE DOCUMENTATION LICENSE

with "1492." Taking a liking to the immigrant, on the Italian's fourth attempt the judge asked him when Columbus had discovered America, and the man could correctly answer "1492." The judge then granted him citizenship.

However touching Brecht's tale, that's not what God did. He didn't change the law to meet us in our fallen condition. No, instead He bore in Himself its full brunt, the full intensity of its violation. But again we ask: *Why not change the law rather than be punished by it?* Could the answer be that God deemed His law so sacred, so inviolable, that He wouldn't alter it no matter what the cost to Himself?

THE CROSS REVEALS THE LAW'S IMMUTABILITY

What else explains the cross, on which God, like the king of Antinomia (second version), underwent punishment for the violation of a law that He could have, had He chosen to, changed? The death of Jesus proves that far from negating or abrogating the law, the cross of Christ reveals its immutability, its eternal perpetuity. Even though (as we saw) we can't be saved by the law, that doesn't mean it has been abolished or revised.

On the contrary. After the cross, were lying, murder, adultery, and stealing suddenly no longer sinful? If the law defines sin, then unless the definition has changed, or unless sin no longer exists, then God's law must still remain valid.

Centuries ago Irish satirist Jonathan Swift wrote: "But will any man say that if the words *drinking, cheating, lying, stealing* were by Act of Parliament ejected out of the English tongue and dictionaries, we should all awake next morning chaste and temperate, honest and just, and lovers of truth? Is this a fair consequence?"[6]

> If God changed His law, then the definition of sin must have altered too.

In the same way, if God's law has been terminated, then why are lying, murder, and stealing still regarded as sinful or wrong? If God changed His law, then the definition of sin must have altered too. Or if He did away with His law, then He must have done the same with sin as well. If that were the case, why does the New Testament say such things as: "If we confess our sins, He is faithful and just to forgive us our sins and to cleanse us from all unrighteousness. If we say that we have not sinned, we make Him a liar, and His word is not in us" (1 John 1:9, 10)? Or: "But each one is tempted when he is drawn away by his own desires and enticed. Then, when desire has conceived, it gives birth to sin; and sin, when it is full-grown, brings forth death" (James 1:14, 15)? What sin is Scripture talking about? How can there be sin if there is no divine law?

Dietrich Bonhoeffer recognized the relationship of law and gospel.

Both the law and the gospel appear in the New Testament. The law shows what sin is, and the gospel points to the remedy for that sin: the death and resurrection of Jesus. "There can be no preaching of the law without the gospel," German theologian Dietrich Bonhoeffer declared, "and no preaching of the gospel without the law. . . . Whatever the church's word to the world may be, it must always be *both* law and gospel."[7]

If God didn't abrogate, or even alter, the law before Christ died on the cross, why do it afterward? It would have been like the king of Antinomia changing the law about vandalizing that statue *after* he, the king himself, had already paid the penalty for the violation. Why not change or abolish it beforehand, and save himself the punishment? In the same way, Jesus' death shows that if the law could've been changed or abrogated, it should've been done so before, not after, the cross. Thus nothing shows the continued validity of the law more than does the death of Jesus, a death that occurred precisely because the law *couldn't* be altered.

DEAD CHRISTIANS

"And soon," wrote Russian poet Marina Tsvetaeva, "all of us will sleep under the earth, we who never let each other sleep above it."[8]

Valid point. Soon we who make so much noise above the earth will sleep under it, noiselessly as well, at least to human ears (decomposition, for sure, occurs in soft decibels, and dirt's a good muffler). And that's everyone now, even those who believe in Jesus, who have His perfect record credited to themselves, who have claimed, by faith, all the New Testament promises of eternal life, such as:

- "Whoever eats My flesh and drinks My blood has eternal life" (John 6:54).
- "And I give them eternal life" (John 10:28).
- "Who shall not receive many times more in this present time, and in the world to come eternal life" (Luke 18:30).
- "For God so loved the world that He gave His only begotten Son, that whoever believes in Him should not perish but have everlasting life" (John 3:16).
- "These things I have written to you who believe in the name of the Son of God, that you may know that you have eternal life" (1 John 5:13).
- "However, for this reason I obtained mercy, that in me first Jesus Christ might show all longsuffering, as a pattern to those who are going to believe on Him for everlasting life" (1 Timothy 1:16).
- "But whoever drinks of the water that I shall give him will never thirst. But the water that I shall give him will become in him a fountain of water springing up into everlasting life" (John 4:14).
- "But now having been set free from sin, and having become slaves of God, you have your fruit to holiness, and the end, everlasting life" (Romans 6:22).
- "And this is the will of Him who sent Me, that everyone who sees the Son and believes in Him may have everlasting life" (John 6:40).
- "Keep yourselves in the love of God, looking for the mercy of our Lord Jesus Christ unto eternal life" (Jude 21).
- "Most assuredly, I say to you, he who believes in Me has everlasting life" (John 6:47).
- "And this is the promise that He has promised us—eternal life" (1 John 2:25).
- "That having been justified by His grace we should become heirs according to the hope of eternal life" (Titus 3:7).

Graveyards are filled with the bones of both Christians and those who mercilessly murdered them. Nero's are beyond dust, as are the Christians that he fed to the lions. How do we explain their deaths despite all these promises?

The great conqueror, Alexander the Great came across the philosopher Diogenes, who was staring at a pile of human bones.

In death there is no difference between king and slave.

"What are you looking for?" Alexander asked.

"Something that I cannot find," Diogenes replied.

"What's that?"

"The difference between your father's bones and those of his slaves."

The difference won't be much—a quantitative (not qualitative) one at best. We might live radically different lives, but in death we're all heading in the same direction, devolving into the stuff out of which we first came. Given enough time, we'll all be nothing but physics' formulas.

On the Fast Track Toward the Ground

Contrary to popular belief, the Bible doesn't teach that the dead soar off to either immediate bliss or eternal torment (see next chapter). Instead, it presents what it taught from the beginning, even from the Garden of Eden, when, after humanity first sinned, God told Adam that he would work by the sweat of his brow "till you return to the ground, for out of it you were taken; for dust you are, and to dust you shall return" (Genesis 3:19). That goes not just for Adam, but for all of us. Who needs faith to believe God's words here? From conception onward, we're on the fast track toward the ground. Life at times can seem like nothing but keeping ourselves preoccupied until we make that final journey back to our origins.

Which raises the question What's all this talk of redemption, of salvation, and of eternal life if we're all just dead men and women walking? As we've seen, we're all sinners, having all violated God's law, so we all stand charged by it. But that's precisely why Jesus came: to save us from the condemnation that our violation of the law brings. And He did it by keeping the law perfectly and then offering to us His perfect record, which becomes ours when we claim it for ourselves. As a result, our condemnation is revoked, and we have all those promises, such as those listed above, of eternal life.

> The godliest saint's just as dead as the ungodliest sinner.

But what do these promises mean if Christians, those who follow Jesus, die just as everyone else does, and if at death we all return to the dust? From what we see now, there's no difference. The godliest saint's just as dead as the ungodliest sinner. How do we, then, understand the promises of salvation, redemption, and eternal life?

Good questions—good enough to deserve answers just as good.

---

[1] Ellen G. White, *Steps to Christ* (Mountain View, Calif.: Pacific Press Pub. Assn., 1956), p. 62.

[2] Arthur Schopenhauer, *The World as Will and Idea* (London: J. M. Dent, 1995), p. 216.

[3] John R. W. Stott, *The Cross of Christ* (Downers Grove, Ill.: InterVarsity Press, 1986), p. 159.

[4] Charles Dickens, *A Tale of Two Cities* (New York: Bantam Classics, 2003), p. 382.

[5] Kenneth Morgan, ed., *The Oxford History of Britain* (Oxford, Eng.: Oxford University Press, 1984), p. 282.

[6] Jonathan Swift, *A Modest Proposal and Other Satires* (Amherst, N.Y.: Prometheus Books, 1995), p. 205.

[7] Dietrich Bonhoeffer, *Ethics* (New York: Collier Books, 1955), pp. 357, 358.

[8] Marina Tsvetaeva, *Selected Poems* (New York: Penguin Books, 1994), p. 3.

THE GREAT CONTROVERSY

WASTE OF SPACE

It's the kind of family found on about every American block: a divorced mom with three children. Living in a suburban housing tract, the kids, 5, 10, and 14, fight, make messes, and fib their way from one trouble to another. Hardly role models, hardly nascent criminals, hardly unique. Mary, their mother, loves her kids but indulges them a bit much. The pain of her recent divorce—with dad (whom the kids miss) off

Steven Spielberg

Radio telescopes have opened new insights into the nature of the universe.

in Mexico accompanied by someone named Sally—remains written large on her face.

Nothing out of the ordinary, at least not until the night that 10-year-old Elliott encounters an extraterrestrial scrounging for food in the garden shed. The creature got accidentally left behind when his spaceship hurriedly left earth. Unlike the hideous and malevolent creatures of H. G. Wells' *War of the Worlds*, this being, whom Elliott and his siblings dub E.T., is a benign, kind, and loving being who simply wants to get home. The kids befriend him, bond with him, and hide him from government agents. By the story's end, the kids, mom included, outwit the government until a spaceship picks up E.T. and he escapes.

Of course, that's science-fiction fantasy (in this case, Steven Spielberg's 1982 move *E.T.*), and that's because there's no such thing as beings from other worlds who reach earth and interact with us here, right?

Well . . . ?

For starters, the universe's a pretty big place. It seems an infinite cosmos for just one inhabitable planet, and not a very big one to boot. It's certainly possible that earth's the only place with life, but if so, it would seem like such an such immense waste, would it not?

That it would, indeed—which is precisely why many scientists believe that other life forms exist beyond the earth. They just don't know how to find them yet, that's all. But it doesn't mean that they aren't trying.

SETI

Known as Drake's equation, it goes like this: you multiply the rate of star formation in our galaxy by the fraction of those stars that have planets. Next you multiply that number by the average number of those planets that can, *potentially*, support life. Afterward, you multiply that product by the fraction of those planets that can actually develop life, and then you multiply that number by the fraction of those that can develop *intelligent* life. Then you multiply that by the fraction of those planets whose intelligent life is willing to communicate with us. Finally, you multiply that number by the fraction of those planets' lives that the communicating civilizations are expected to occupy.

What's all the number-crunching about? It's about estimating how many planets with life could, conceivably, communicate with earth. When the ciphering's done, Drake's equation

$$N = N^* \; f_p \; n_e \; f_l \; f_i \; f_c \; f_L$$

N^* represents the number of stars in the Milky Way Galaxy.

f_p is the fraction of stars that have planets around them.

n_e is the number of planets per star that are capable of sustaining life.

f_l is the fraction of planets in n_e on which life evolves.

f_i is the fraction of f_l on which intelligent life evolves.

f_c is the fraction of f_i that communicate.

f_L is the fraction of the existences of f_c during which the communicating civilizations live.

When all of these variables are multiplied together, we come up with:

N the number of communicating civilizations in the galaxy.

computes about 10,000 (give or take a few) communicative extraterrestrial planets in our galaxy. That's just our neck of the woods, now. If 10,000 or so is an average per galaxy, and billions of galaxies exist out there . . . well, you do the math. We're hardly home alone in the universe.

Which makes sense. However well-suited the cosmos is for human life, why would the God depicted in Scripture as having created all things ("For by Him all things were created that are in heaven and that are on earth, visible and invisible" [Colossians 1:16]) establish life only here and nowhere else? Sure, with all the unpleasantness of our planet (diseases, war, nukes, missiles, pop stars) one could understand God putting a little space between us and our neighbors, *but creating the entire cosmos just to house us?* Though possible, it just doesn't seem reasonable, that's all.

No Cosmic Joke

Which is why scientists, for years now, have been scanning the heavens for extraterrestrial life. Putting aside any theological considerations, there seems to be enough scientific evidence to substantiate

PUBLIC DOMAIN

Astronomers have discovered that our solar system is not the only place in which a star has a family of planets circling it.

the possibility of life elsewhere. "I view this universe not as a 'cosmic joke,'" said one Nobel prize laureate, "but as a meaningful entity—made in such a way as to generate life and mind, bound to give birth to thinking beings able to discern truth, apprehend beauty, feel love, yearn after goodness, define evil, experience mystery."[1] Just here on earth, or elsewhere, too?

Since 1984 the SETI (Search for Extraterrestrial Intelligence) Institute has been scanning the sky, looking for life outside our earthly borders.

The branch of science known as astrobiology seeks to explore the possibility of cosmic life. NASA has its own astrobiology institute, and its Web site reads: "Astrobiology is devoted to the scientific study of life in the universe—its origins, evolution, distribution, and future. . . . Does life exist on worlds other than Earth? How could terrestrial life potentially survive and adapt beyond our home planet?"[2]

Since 1984 the SETI (Search for Extraterrestrial Intelligence) Institute has been scanning the sky, looking for life outside our earthly borders. "The purpose of the Institute," it says about itself, "as defined at that time and still true today, is to conduct scientific research and educational projects relevant to the origin, nature, prevalence, and distribution of life in the universe. . . . Today the SETI Institute Board of Trustees counts among its 18 members two Nobel Prize winners, four members of the National Academy of Sciences, one member of the National Academy of Engineering, and several current and former Fortune 500 business executives. This strong scientific guidance, combined with extraordinary business and technology leadership, enables the Trustees to help the organization advance scientifically while securing an enduring financial foundation for the future."[3]

This isn't UFO and Trekkie kook stuff. Rather it's serious science using the best technology in an attempt to discover what reason leads them to believe could be there: extraterrestrial life.

EXTRATERRESTRIALS

Now, while award-winning scientists and astronomers are pointing fancy radio telescopes toward the sky in hope of retrieving an intelligent peep or mutter from the heavens, the Bible not only talks about the existence of extraterrestrial life but has given us some fascinating insights into what it is like. Beside the reality of God Himself, Scripture makes clear what science (however different its approach) suspects: earth isn't the only place in creation with intelligent life. On the contrary.

Keep in mind that when the Bible talks about "heaven" or the "heavens," it's not necessarily always referring to heaven as a place where God exists (though it sometimes is), but to the cosmos itself, such as in Genesis 15:5, which reads: "Then He brought him outside and said, 'Look now *toward heaven,* and count *the stars* if you are able to number them.'" Or Deuteronomy 4:19: "And take heed lest you lift your eyes to *heaven, and when you see the sun, the moon, and the stars,* all the host of heaven, you feel driven to worship them and serve them, which the Lord your God has given to all the peoples under the whole heaven." In these and other texts "heaven" represents the cosmos itself.

©PHOTODISC

Astronomers are pointing fancy radio telescopes toward the sky in hope of retrieving an intelligent peep or mutter from the heavens.

What, then, does the Bible say about life in the universe and its interaction with our planet?

COSMIC STRUGGLE IN SCRIPTURE

- "His intent was that now, through the church, the manifold wisdom of God should be made known to the rulers and authorities in the heavenly realms" (Ephesians 3:10, NIV).

- "For we do not wrestle against flesh and blood, but against principalities, against powers, against the rulers of the darkness of this age, against spiritual hosts of wickedness in the heavenly places" (Ephesians 6:12).

- "For by Him all things were created that are in heaven and that are on earth, visible and invisible, whether thrones or dominions or principalities or powers. All things were created through Him and for Him" (Colossians 1:16).

- "Where were you when I laid the foundations of the earth? Tell Me, if you have understanding. Who determined its measurements? Surely you know! Or who stretched the line upon it? To what were its foundations fastened? Or who laid its cornerstone, when the morning stars sang together, and all the sons of God shouted for joy?" (Job 38:4-7).

- "Now there was a day when the sons of God came to present themselves before the Lord, and Satan also came among them. And the Lord said to Satan, 'From where do you come?' So Satan answered the Lord and said, 'From going to and fro in the earth, and from walking back and forth on it'" (Job 1:6, 7).

- "And war broke out in heaven: Michael and his angels fought with the dragon; and the dragon and his angels fought, but they did not prevail, nor was a place found for them in heaven any longer. So the great dragon was cast out, that serpent of old, called the Devil and Satan, who deceives the whole world; he was cast to the earth, and his angels were cast out with him. . . . Therefore rejoice, O heavens, and you who dwell in them! Woe to the inhabitants of the earth and of the sea! For the devil is come down to you, having great wrath, because he knows that he has a short time" (Revelation 12:7-12).

- "For I think that God has displayed us, the apostles, last, as men condemned to death; for we have been made a spectacle to the world, both to angels and to men" (1 Corinthians 4:9).

- "Be sober, be vigilant; because your adversary the devil walks about like a roaring lion, seeking whom he may devour" (1 Peter 5:8).

- "Now behold, an angel of the Lord stood by him, and a light shone in the prison: and he struck Peter on the side and raised him up, saying, 'Arise quickly!' And his chains fell off his hands" (Acts 12:7).

- "Do not forget to entertain strangers, for by so doing some have unwittingly entertained angels" (Hebrews 13:2).

What, then, does the Bible say about life in the cosmos?

It's there, and (what's more) it interacts with our world, too.

THE GREAT CONTROVERSY

When young Isaac Newton, sitting under the apple tree, got clunked on the noggin, he had the most astonishing insight: the force that propelled the apple onto his head, gravity, was the same force that kept the moon in orbit around earth, and earth in orbit around the sun. And though for Newton the idea that "one body may act upon another at a distance through a vacuum without the mediation of anything else" was "so great an absurdity that I believe no man who has in philosophical matters any competent faculty of thinking can ever fall into it,"[4] he knew that gravity did just that—"act upon another at a distance through a vacuum"—however inexplicable the phenomenon might be.

It gets even more amazing: not only does all matter have a gravitational pull—all matter has a gravitational effect on all other matter. Thus you exert a gravitational influence not just on your cat but on the moon, the sun, even faraway stars. That influence is, to be sure, negligible, but it's real. Your existence, literally, touches the entire measurable cosmos.

The point? When your very physical presence can cause even a little tug on the Crab Nebulae, then the universe itself, no matter how big, is more tightly linked than what our earthbound experience alone might suggest. When the Bible, therefore, talks not only about the existence of life in other parts of the creation but claims that some of this life is involved with us here, it's not something that should be that hard to accept, not with what we know about all matter in the cosmos influencing all matter. That we can exert a gravitational pull (however tiny) on another part of the universe

Isaac Newton

hardly proves that beings from other parts of the cosmos can interact with life here. But it does suggest, by analogy, that the idea of one part of the universe influencing another is not far-fetched. On the contrary, it's basic physics.

ANGELS COME TO EARTH

And basic Bible theology, too. What the texts cited above reveal is that not only does life exist elsewhere in the cosmos but that some of it, beings known as angels, have come to earth and are exerting an influence here even if we can't see them any more than we can the millions of cell phone calls pulsing through the air right in front of our eyes.

Poet William Blake once wrote about the link between heaven and earth: "A Skylark wounded in the wing, /A Cherubim does cease to sing."[5] And though that's a bit much, it's not too far off from the kind of reality that the Bible does depict: other intelligent beings exist in the universe, and not only are they interested in what's happening on earth (we have been made a spectacle to the whole universe), but some are directly involved in what goes on here.

Though Scripture doesn't get explicit, it does reveal a struggle between good and evil—a great controversy, we might say—that began in another part of the cosmos but now rages here.

Scripture depicts a war in heaven, in another part of the cosmos—a battle between angels; and (according to the texts) the losers, Satan and his angels, were exiled to our world, where the conflict continues, only now with us involved. Taking these passages, along with ones that show other angels friendly toward us (such as Acts 12:7; Daniel 6:22; Psalm 34:7), we can see that according to the Bible we on earth are in the midst of a spiritual battle

"A Skylark wounded in the wing, A Cherubim does cease to sing."

between agencies of good and evil. That we might not see these beings themselves hardly proves that they aren't there or that the conflict's not real any more than the fact that we can't see electromagnetic radiation means that it's not real either.

COME ON!

Sure, many people, particularly in the secularized West, quickly laugh off the idea of angels, demons, and the supernatural. But that doesn't mean that such beings don't exist—only how heavily influenced many are by the rationalistic scientific worldview that limits all reality only to what we can explain through natural and quantifiable law, an idea that goes back to the Enlightenment.

> Though Scripture doesn't get explicit, it does reveal a struggle between good and evil that began in another part of the cosmos but now rages here.

"No explanation from without," Ernst Cassirer commented about the Enlightenment ideal, "which seeks the principle of nature in a realm beyond, can ever achieve its aim. For man is the work of nature, and he has no existence except in nature. . . . All the process of nature, including those commonly called 'intellectual,' the whole physical and moral order of things, are reducible to matter and motion and are completely explicable in terms of these two concepts."[6]

Matter and motion alone—that explains everything? If so, then love, courage, honor, passion, beauty, and art are just matter and motion, atoms and molecules, nothing more? We're only "systems," purely physical processes run by purely physical laws? Equations in flesh and blood, beings whose whole existence can be reduced to math and formulas alone, like the motion of stars?

"Unfortunately," philosopher Michael Polanyi observed, "the *ideal* goals of science are nonsensical. Current biology is based on the assumption that you can explain the processes of life in terms of physics and chemistry; and, of course, physics and chemistry are both to be represented ultimately in terms of the forces acting between atomic particles. So all life, all human beings, and all works of man, including Shakespeare's sonnets and Kant's *Critique of Pure Reason*, are also to be so represented. The ideal of science remains . . . to replace all human knowledge by complete knowledge of atoms in motion."[7]

A BROADER VIEW OF REALITY

The Bible, however, give us a broader view of reality, one not hemmed in by the narrow constraints of science and its atomistic view of existence. Scripture doesn't deny such physical processes. On the contrary, the opening chapter of Genesis depicts the moon and the sun and stars, not as deities or gods (as in the pagan religions of that time), but as physical inanimate objects subject to basic laws of nature. What Scripture doesn't do, however, is limit reality to those fundamental natural laws. Instead it points to God, who is both greater than nature and above it.

Again, a purely naturalistic view of all creation isn't logical. As we have already pointed out, something outside of nature, beyond nature, and greater than nature would have to exist for nature to somehow arise out of it, in the same way that something outside a painting, beyond a painting, and greater than a painting would have had to have created it. The *Mona Lisa* was no more preexisting in Leonardo da

> The *Mona Lisa* was no more preexisting in Leonardo da Vinci's paintbrush than *Crime and Punishment* lurked hidden in Fyodor Dostoyevsky's pen.

Vinci's paintbrush than *Crime and Punishment* lurked hidden in Fyodor Dostoyevsky's pen.

The Bible does point to sentient beings who exist in realms not limited by our present scientific and rationalistic views of the physical world (views that, by the way, are constantly changing). Few in the Western world would question the reality of good and evil even though we cannot reduce it to scientific processes and laws, and most would recognize an ongoing struggle between the two perspectives. Many of those beings (angels) that Scripture tells us are involved in that conflict—though first existing in another part of the cosmos—are now here. Some are friendly,

Da Vinci's *Mona Lisa* did not lurk hidden in his paintbrush.

others hostile, and all are involved in that colossal battle between good and evil, a conflict that started somewhere else in the cosmos but now rages among, in, and through us. And though we might not perceive those beings directly, we clearly recognize the results of their interaction here, just as we might not see radio waves but can witness their results (such as every time we answer a cell phone call, turn on a TV, or use wireless Internet connections).

GOOD VERSUS EVIL

And what are the results of this battle, the cosmic warfare between good and evil? For millennia people have watched this struggle play out, no matter how hidden the supernatural forces behind it.

Many centuries before Christ the Zoroastrian religion taught about supernatural forces of good and evil locked in battle, a theme picked up in the earlier centuries A.D. by Manicheans, who also believed in a supernatural battle between good and evil, light and darkness.

As we have already noted, one doesn't need religion to observe the reality of this struggle. Friedrich Nietzsche, the hardest atheist of his era, declared: "Let us conclude. The two *opposing* values 'good and bad,' 'good and evil' have been engaged in a fearful struggle on earth for thousands of years."[8] And T. S. Eliot wrote about the "perpetual struggle" between good and evil.[9]

Who doesn't sense this battle between good and evil even on a personal level? We may not be able to articulate it or understand it clearly, but we recognize that it plays out in our hearts, in our own daily activities, and in choices and temptations, however fuzzy the issues and forces behind them often appear.

German poet Goethe, in his poem *Faust*, has the main character say:
"Two souls, alas, are dwelling in my breast,
And either would be severed from its brother;
The one holds fast with joyous earthly lust
Onto the world of man with organs clinging;
The other soars impassioned from the dust,
To the realms of lofty forebears winging."[10]

This struggle isn't just something that we imagine or the result of culture and subjectivity alone, however much custom and culture factor in. Behind our senses, which give us such a thin slice of reality (like trying to learn about the electronic intricacies of a CD player if all you ever have access to is the music that comes out of it), there rages a vast conflict between good and evil, between Christ and Satan, constantly playing itself out at every level of human existence, from the interplay of nations to the quiet struggles deep in every human soul, and the issues are of eternal consequences.

Johann Wolfgang von Goethe

VYING FOR SUPREMACY

"Through no choice of our own, we exist in a world in which good and evil, right and wrong, law and lawlessness, dignity and dishonor, faith and unbelief vie for supremacy. Every day our thoughts, actions, and words place us on one side or another in this great spiritual conflict. However complicated its manifestations appear, however blurry, fuzzy, and gray our moral options, choices, and decisions seem—there are only two sides, only two choices: good and evil, truth and error, right and wrong. As with life and death, there's no middle ground, however much we fool ourselves into thinking that's where we stand."[11]

How could evil arise in a universe created and governed by a God who, as the Bible says, is "love"?

Even if one accepts (as millions do) the idea of Satan and his fall, and of supernatural powers battling here on earth, though, it raises even more questions, the most obvious being: If God is the Creator of all things, then where did Satan come from? If, as many Christians believe, evil started somewhere else in the universe with Satan, it only begs the question: How could evil arise in a universe created and governed by a God who, as the Bible says, is "love"?

Good questions. And we can go to the Bible to find clues to their answers.

LUCIFER'S FALL

"You were the anointed cherub who covers; I established you; you were on the holy mountain of God; you walked back and forth in the midst of fiery stones. You were perfect in your ways from the day you were created, till iniquity was found in you" (Ezekiel 28:14, 15).

"How you are fallen from heaven, O Lucifer, son of the morning! How you are cut down to the ground, you who weakened the nations! For you have said in your heart: 'I will ascend into heaven, I will exalt my throne above the stars of God: I will also sit on the mount of the congregation on the farthest sides of the north: I will ascend above the heights of the clouds, I will be like the Most High'" (Isaiah 14:12-14).

> "You [Lucifer] were perfect in your ways from the day you were created, till iniquity was found in you" (Ezekiel 28:15).

These five verses reveal a wealth of knowledge that all scientific experimentation and philosophical speculation could never uncover any more than X-raying an original folio of *Hamlet* could disclose the secret of Shakespeare's genius.

For centuries biblical commentators have understood the passages as referring to the supernatural being Satan and to his fall—the fall depicted in the book of Revelation (12:7-9). But, again, how did this evil being arise? If, as Scripture says, "for by Him [God] all things were created that are in heaven and that are on earth, visible and invisible, whether thrones or dominions or principalities or powers. All things were created through Him and for Him" (Colossians 1:16), then "all things" must include "that serpent of old, called the Devil and Satan" (Revelation 12:9). How could that be?

We find the answer, in part, in Ezekiel 28:15, which—talking about Satan—said that he "was perfect in [his] ways from the day [he was] created, till iniquity was found in [him]." Notice that Satan was "perfect" when a perfect God brought him into being. And yet iniquity eventually appeared in him? How could that be?

Because "perfect" must include *moral* freedom, the ability to become evil. Otherwise, how could a being—"perfect" in his ways, even from his origin—become so? If he was perfect from the start, then iniquity wasn't initially there. It came later, which meant that, whatever "perfect" means, it includes the *potential* for turning evil.

But couldn't God have created a being that didn't have such danger? He could have, but at what cost to that being? Could such a creature—one with no moral options—even be "perfect"?

What God Cannot Do

After years of oppression, poverty, and forced obscurity by the Soviet government, the poet Anna Akhmatova was allowed a poetry reading in 1944 at the largest auditorium in Moscow, the Polytechnic Museum. When she finished, the audience of 3,000 rose to their feet and gave her thundering applause. When told about what happened that night, Joseph Stalin replied, "Who organized this standing ovation?"

How sad that Stalin lived in such a fake environment that it even preprogrammed and prearranged spontaneity. What good are praises if those doing the praising are forced to do it?

PUBLIC DOMAIN

Russian poet Anna Akhmatova

Imagine a scientific genius that we'll call Dr. Ralph. Obsessed with his work, he never married, had a family, or enjoyed any close loving ties since childhood. As he enters his last years, he's feeling the pain of a lonely and loveless existence, and so—being the genius that he is—he creates a robot that looks, acts, and feels just like a human being. He makes it into the image of a young beautiful woman that he names Carla. She caters to his every whim, desire, and need, including expressions and manifestations of love. Carla is everything that any man would ever desire, without any of the problems that any relationship would normally encounter. Yet no matter how many times Carla tells Dr. Ralph she loves him, no matter all the things she does to express love, Dr. Ralph realizes that, in the end, it means nothing, for no matter what Carla says or does, it cannot be true love, because he had programmed it in her.

In other words, love has to be free, or it can't be love. What Dr. Ralph learned from his creation was that love cannot be forced, not even by God Himself.

> **Omnipotence doesn't mean the ability to do what's logically impossible within the confines and limits and definitions of the reality that God has created.**

Indeed, contrary to popular notions about God's omnipotence, there are certain things that He cannot do. However dumb the question "Can God create a rock so big that He can't lift it?" it nevertheless presents a deep truth: Within the parameters of this universe, at least as God has created it, logical limitations exist on what He can do. Omnipotence doesn't mean the ability to do what's logically impossible within the confines and limits and definitions of the reality that God has created.

For example, can He make a whole positive number that's less than zero? Not in this universe—at least not as we understand the definitions of "positive," "whole," "number," "less," and "zero." Can God create a married bachelor? No, not within the current definitions of "married" and "bachelor." Or can God create a circle that's made of right angles? Again, no, not as long as we hold to our present concepts of "circle" and "right angles." Within the confines of this creation, certain logical and linguistic limitations exist, even for God.

LOVE MUST HAVE A CHOICE

This is crucial. It gets to the übermetaphysic of Christianity, which is: Could God create a forced love? Can someone be compelled to love against his or her will? "Without choice," wrote theologian Francis Schaeffer, "the word *love* is meaningless."[12] Can love be programmed or wired into someone in a way that the individual has no choice other than to love, such as with Carla, Dr. Ralph's robot?

Of course not. Love, by its nature and definition, must be freely given, or not at all. Even God cannot force love, because the moment

He does so, it's no longer love. The Lord can no more force love than He can create a rock so big that He can't lift it.

How ironic. People argue that if "God is love" (1 John 4:8), why evil and suffering? Yet it's precisely because "God is love" that evil exists. Not because love demands the existence of evil (far from it!), but because love requires a moral environment of freedom, and freedom by its nature as freedom, especially moral freedom, requires the potential to do wrong as well as good. Otherwise there's no morality or freedom at all.

If Satan was created a "perfect" being, then His perfection included a moral component. Perhaps the definition of "perfect" in God's universe demands such a moral component. Yet to truly be moral a being must have the potential to be immoral. We could design a robot that's trained and programmed to save people in burning buildings, to help elderly women cross the street, and to rescue drowning children, but that robot wouldn't be any more moral than a traffic light (which keeps cars from crashing into each other at an intersection) is moral.

The Lord can no more force love than He can create a rock so big that He can't lift it.

Thus Satan, a being created with the freedom to make moral choices, obviously abused that freedom and went astray.

What happened? And how?

Again, for the answer, we go to the Bible.

REIGN IN HELL OR SERVE IN HEAVEN?

Plutarch once gave this account of the great Roman leader Julius Caesar.

"There is a story," he wrote, "that while [Caesar] was crossing the Alps he came to a small native village with hardly any inhabitants and altogether a miserable-looking place. His friends were laughing and joking about it, saying: 'No doubt here too one would find people pushing themselves forward to gain office, and here too there are struggles to get the first place and jealous rivalries among the great men.' Caesar then said to them in all seriousness: 'As far as I am concerned, I would rather be the first man here than the second in Rome.'"[13]

PUBLIC DOMAIN

Julius Caesar

What's with us? No matter what we have, if someone—even just one individual—has more, or has it better, then we fixate on that individual until a loud ringing in our ears blocks out everything else, even the sounds of the thousands, maybe millions, who have less than we do or even nothing at all. It was like that with Caesar and, apparently, with Satan, too.

Scripture, as is so often the case, doesn't give details, but according to some of the texts we've seen, something similar happened to this "anointed cherub" who was "on the holy mountain of God" (Ezekiel 28:14)—words understood to denote a high position, one close to God Himself. Satan, whatever he was, was an exalted creature. Yet for this free moral being that still wasn't enough.

"How you are fallen from heaven, O Lucifer, son of the morning!

How you are cut down to the ground, you who weakened the nations! For you have said in your heart: 'I will ascend into heaven, I will exalt my throne above the stars of God; I will sit also on the mount of the congregation on the farthest sides of the north; I will ascend above the heights of the clouds, I will be like the Most High'" (Isaiah 14:12-14).

Whatever his station, Lucifer wanted even more. By aspiring to be like the Most High Himself, He in essence sought to *be* God. Yet a created being is not God, nor could ever be, any more than a poker hand, no matter how good, could ever become a poker player.

> **Poet John Milton in *Paradise Lost* caught the essence of Satan's spirit when he had the devil declare: "Better to reign in hell, than serve in heav'n."**

Again, God created moral beings in a moral universe with moral freedom. Such moral freedom included the options of jealously, ambition, pride, and the desire to be more than we can ever be. Otherwise how could a being, "perfect in [his] ways" (Ezekiel 28:15), desire to be the Creator other than if "perfection" included the potential to do just that?

Poet John Milton in *Paradise Lost* caught the essence of Satan's spirit when he had the devil declare: "Better to reign in hell, than serve in heav'n."[14]

And not just Lucifer had this potential—other heavenly beings did as well. We know this because Scripture alludes to other angels who allied themselves with Lucifer. It apparently got so bad that a war in heaven (the one we have already looked at in Revelation 12:7-12) began.

Satan's desire to have more than was rightfully his led to his downfall and that of other angels, those who joined his side in a cosmic war that, though starting in another part of the universe, now plays out here on earth.

In fact, this same sentiment that worked against him in the perfect environment of heaven worked in a perfect earth. The biblical depiction of the fall of Adam and Eve (Genesis 3) again demonstrates the moral freedom of all of God's rational and intelligent creatures, and goes a long way in explaining how evil could arise in a universe created by an all-knowing, all-loving deity.

FREEDOM IN EDEN

"In the beginning God created the heavens and the earth" (Genesis 1:1). Not only did God create them—He made them perfect. Throughout the creation process God would look at what He had done and make a judgment on it. Scripture expressed it like this:

- "And God saw the light, that it was good" (Genesis 1:4).

- "And God called the dry land Earth, and the gathering together of the waters He called Seas. And God saw that it was good" (verse 10).

- "And the earth brought forth grass, the herb that yields seed according to its kind, and the tree that yields fruit, whose seed is in itself according to its kind. And God saw that it was good" (verse 12).

- "God set them in the firmament of the heavens to give light on the earth, and to rule over the day and over the night, and to divide the light from the darkness. And God saw that it was good" (verses 17, 18).

- "So God created great sea creatures and every living thing that moves, with which the waters abounded, according to their kind, and every winged bird according to its kind. And God saw that it was good" (verse 21).

- "And God made the beast of the earth according to its kind, cattle according to its kind, and everything that creeps on the earth according to its kind. And God saw that it was good" (verse 25).

- "Then God saw everything that He had made, and indeed it was very good" (verse 31).

And that "everything" included Adam and Eve, the first two people, whom Scripture depicts as created, directly and purposely, by God. "So God created man in His own image; in the image of God He created him; male and female He created them" (verse 27).

A perfect God makes a perfect creation, a "very good" one. In addition, the two humans were unlike anything else in that creation, made "in His own image; in the image of God." For centuries people have debated the significance of the phrase "in the image of God." Whatever it means, it must at least indicate that humans are a step "above" the rest of the earthly creation, that at least there's something higher, "better," unique about humans that sets them apart from, say, the seashells, the trees, and "everything that creeps on the earth" (verse 25)—a uniqueness that's pretty obvious, even today.

Thus Adam and Eve must have come flawless from the hand of their Creator. How could a perfect God do anything else, especially with beings made in His own image? In this sense they're like Lucifer, "perfect in your ways from the day you were created." Should one expect anything less from Adam and Eve, beings made "in the image of God," an attribute that Scripture never applies to Lucifer, even before his fall?

Now comes the famous section of the Bible in which God warns Adam about eating from the tree of the knowledge of good and evil. "And the Lord God commanded the man, saying, 'Of every tree of the garden you may freely eat; but of the tree of the knowledge of good and evil you shall not eat, for in the day that you eat of it you shall surely die'" (Genesis 2:16, 17).

> **Adam and Eve must have come flawless from the hand of their Creator. How could a perfect God do anything else, especially with beings made in His own image?**

Forests have been felled to supply the paper used for all the commentary on these verses. We, however, will concentrate on one point: the moral freedom of Adam and Eve as revealed in this account.

MORAL CAPACITY TO CHOOSE

Why would God warn them about doing something unless they had the moral capacity to choose what He told them specifically *not* to do? If He didn't want them to eat from it, He could have, when making them, programmed their brains in a way that would have made Adam and Eve avoid the tree the way we, today, are programmed to avoid hunger, thirst, or pain. Or He could have placed the tree in an environment in which it was impossible for them to get at it. He could have put it on the moon, or somewhere else out of reach. Perhaps God could have made it undesirable, something that would have repulsed them. Finally, He could have not created the tree at all, removing any possibility of them sampling it (you can't eat the fruit of a nonexistent tree). But He did none of these things, a fact that implies two crucial points:

> **Adam and Eve were free moral beings, capable of obeying or disobeying their Maker.**

1. Adam and Eve were free moral beings, capable of obeying or disobeying their Maker. That was, specifically, how God created them. Their capacity for freedom is obvious, because otherwise, why would God have warned them about doing something they were incapable of?

2. The tree was a test. Why would the Lord have placed it there, within the reach of beings who had the capacity to obey or disobey, unless He meant to test them with it by giving them the opportunity to show their allegiance as free moral creatures? We have here two moral beings, endowed with free choice, who faced a test of their loyalty to the one who created them, a test of what they would do with their freedom.

We can see the conflict motif between God and Satan played out in what comes next, because "that serpent of old, called the Devil and Satan," appears in Eden, in this perfect environment created by a perfect God. According to Genesis, Eve is near the tree that God had forbidden them to eat from when Satan appears.

"And he [the serpent] said to the woman, 'Has God indeed said, "You shall not eat of every tree of the garden?"' And the woman said to the serpent, 'We may eat of the fruit of the trees of the garden; but of the fruit of the tree which is in the midst of the garden, God has said, "You shall not eat it, nor shall you touch it, lest you die."' Then the serpent said to the woman, 'You will not surely die. For God knows that in the day you eat of it your eyes will be opened, and you will be like God, knowing good and evil.' So when the woman saw that the tree was good for food, that it was pleasant to the eyes, and a tree desirable to make one wise, she took of its fruit and ate. She also gave to her husband with her, and he ate" (Genesis 3:1-6).

THE DESIRE TO BE GOD

Two more points:

First, we notice a conflict between what God and Satan each say. God declared, *Don't eat; you will die,* while Satan claimed, *Eat; you won't die.* Here, subtly, we catch a glimpse of the conflict between God and Satan, one now being played out on earth through Eve, who has to choose between two voices—that of God, who said not to eat of the tree, and that of the serpent, who tells her to, even though she knows God's command. (After all, she said, flat out: "But of the fruit of the tree which is in the midst of the garden, God has said, 'You shall not eat it, nor shall you touch it, lest you die.'") She couldn't plead ignorance.

Second, and most fascinating, is how Satan manipulated her. "You will not surely die. For God knows that in the day you eat of it your eyes will be opened, and you will be like God, knowing good and evil." (Other Bible versions translate it "You shall be as gods" since the Hebrew word here for "God" has a plural form.)

Satan, in heaven, wanted to be "like the Most High." Now in Eden he tempts Eve with the same bait, this desire to be "like God." Amazingly enough, she—as we'll see—took the bait, because apparently something inside her wanted to be "like God." How ironic, because she already was "like God" in that—unlike any of the other newly formed creatures—she and her husband had been made "in the image of God." Yet, as with Lucifer, no matter what she already had, it still wasn't enough, and, according to the biblical texts, she and her husband both ate.

What is it about the creature, even in heavenly and Edenic perfection, that seeks to be the Creator, that wants to say in its heart: "I will be like the Most High"? It seems to be a continuing problem.

> **"The sin of man is that he seeks to make himself God."**

"The sin of man," theologian Reinhold Niebuhr observed, "is that he seeks to make himself God."[15]

Atheist apologist Jean-Paul Sartre once wrote that "to be man means to reach toward being God. Or if you prefer, man fundamentally is the desire to be God."[16]

Susan Neiman concludes that "questions about God and His purposes, the nature and sense of Creation, thus the materials for thinking about the problem of evil, are all out of bounds. The wish to answer them is the wish to transcend the limits of human reason. And the wish to transcend those limits is uncomfortably close to the wish to be God."[17]

The apostle Paul, warning about an anti-Christian power that would arise after a time of apostasy in the Christian church, depicted the religious entity as one that would seek to place itself in the role of God, a power that would all but make itself out to be deity. "Let no one deceive you by any means; for that Day will not come unless the falling away comes first, and the man of sin is revealed, the son of perdition, who opposes and exalts himself above all that is called God or that is worshiped, so that he sits as God in the temple of God, showing himself that he is God" (2 Thessalonians 2:3, 4).

Whatever its multiple faces and manifestations, this desire to be God boils down to one thing: *authority*. Who or what is our final authority? In Eden it was a case of whether the first human couple would listen to the direct command of God or heed another authority—in this case, the voice of Satan.

Scripture shows their decision.

THE BOTTOM LINE

"So when the woman saw that the tree was good for food, that it was pleasant to the eyes, and a tree desirable to make one wise, she took of its fruit and ate. She also gave to her husband with her, and he ate" (Genesis 3:6).

The blatant disregard of God's explicit command by two perfect beings who had no excuse whatsoever for their disobedience allowed sin, evil, suffering, and death to infiltrate the world, wrapping themselves into its very fiber. Think of the principle behind what happened to our world. Something went awry at the *beginning*—at the *foundations*—and thus all that was afterward developed upon those foundations went awry as well.

If someone starts building a house, but the foundation is crooked, cracked, or unstable, the rest of the house—everything that rests on that faulty foundation—will be affected negatively as well. Geometry is created from axioms, foundation principles upon which all else sits. If something corrupts those axioms or principles, then all that depends on them will be corrupted as well. When something's ruined in its very essence, then everything else that arises from those degraded elements will also be damaged themselves. How could they not?

©PHOTODISC

> Something went awry at the *beginning*—at the *foundations*—and thus all that was afterward developed upon those foundations went awry as well.

The first two human beings, the parents of the whole race, became corrupted. All who descended from them would share their condition too, just as only out-of-tune music will emerge from an out-of-tune and broken piano. Each generation after Adam and Eve became worse and worse until, as Scripture says, "the Lord saw that the wickedness of man was great in the earth, and that every intent of the thoughts of his heart was only evil continually" (Genesis 6:5).

Only out-of-tune music will emerge from an out-of-tune and broken piano.

When you build a wall, if the angle's off by only a few degrees near the floor, the farther you get from the floor the worse the deviation gets. With humanity, the further from Eden, the further from Adam and Eve's *original* perfection, the more degenerate we become. Here's how Scripture depicts the human situation not many centuries after the Fall: "The earth also was corrupt before God, and the earth was filled with violence. So God looked upon the earth, and indeed it was corrupt; for all flesh had corrupted their way on the earth. And God said to Noah, 'The end of all flesh is come before Me, for the earth is filled with violence through them; and behold, I will destroy them with the earth'" (verses 11-13).

VIEWING NATURE THROUGH DISTORTED VISION

Noah's flood came as a direct result of sin, and who knows how that catastrophe altered the physical processes and equilibrium of God's perfect earth (see Genesis 8:22)? The Fall had already affected nature itself (Genesis 3:16-19), most likely in ways that we can't comprehend, because nature as it now exists is the only one we know, and so we have no baseline to measure it against or to compare it with.

Also, we can view nature only through our own corruption, only through our own warped and twisted senses and consciousness—which means it comes to us about as accurately as the *Mona Lisa* does to a color-blind individual with astigmatism. (It's like those with tainted blood giving themselves a transfusion.) The Fall irrevocably affected our entire planet and all that's on it, and we and our current world are the sad results.

None of us living today saw the fall of Adam and Eve (none of us saw the fall of the ancient Roman Empire, either). Because we were not there, Adam and Eve's transgression is an event that has to be told to us (revealed to us), and it has been—through the Bible. Because we weren't there and didn't see it happen, we must take it on trust—faith. But who needs faith to see the pain, the suffering, the evil, and the death that mauls our planet and impregnates the very fiber of our existence? We require faith, not to recognize the results, but to understand the causes.

How did suffering begin? Scripture, in those opening chapters of Genesis, explains how. Humanity, at its inception, severed itself from its Creator, its only source of life, security, and peace (remember, the world was "very good" before the Fall), choosing instead another authority—and the result was chaos, rebellion, suffering, and death from the start, themes that permeate all life everywhere on our planet. Nothing living on earth is immune to the Fall's consequences.

> Who needs faith to see the pain, the suffering, the evil, and the death that mauls our planet and impregnates the very fiber of our existence?

Through disobedience, our first parents opened the door to evil. By choosing to listen to Satan, as opposed to God, they invited another power into their lives and, by default, into ours. Peter wasn't just being poetic when he warned: "Be sober, be vigilant; because your adversary the devil walks about as a roaring lion, seeking whom he may devour" (1 Peter 5:8). He was pointing to a reality beyond where sense and reason alone can take us.

Sin's the ultimate source of all suffering, because it inevitably leads to pain, evil, and death. We're caught in a war in which supernatural forces of evil battle supernatural forces of good in and through us.

That's the problem.

But Jesus Christ, through what He did on the cross, is the solution.

---

[1] In Paul Davies, "E.T. and God," *Atlantic Monthly,* September 2003, p. 114.

[2] http://nai.arc.nasa.gov/about/about_nai.cfm (November 2005).

[3] http://www.seti.org/site/pp.asp (November 2005).

[4] In Rupert Hall, *Isaac Newton: Adventurer in Thought* (Cambridge, Mass.: Cambridge University Press, 1992), p. 248.

[5] William Blake, "Auguries of Innocence," *Romantic Poets: Blake to Poe* (New York: Viking Press, 1972), p. 18.

[6] Ernst Cassirer, *The Philosophy of the Enlightenment* (Boston: Beacon Press, 1955), pp. 65, 66.

[7] Michael Polanyi and Harry Prosch, *Meaning* (Chicago: University of Chicago Press, 1975), p. 25.

[8] Friedrich Nietzsche, *On the Genealogy of Morals* (New York: Random House, 1967), p. 52.

[9] T. S. Eliot, "The Rock," *The Complete Poems and Plays,* p. 98.

[10] Johann Wolfgang von Goethe, *Faust* (New York: W. W. Norton, 2001), p. 31.

[11] Clifford Goldstein, *The Day Evil Dies* (Hagerstown, Md.: Review and Herald Pub. Assn., 1999), pp. 10, 11.

[12] Francis Schaeffer, *Genesis in Space and Time* (Downers Grove, Ill.: InterVarsity Press, 1979), p. 72.

[13] Plutarch, *Fall of the Roman Republic* (New York: Penguin Classics, 1972), pp. 254, 255.

[14] John Milton, *Paradise Lost* (New York: W. W. Norton, 1975), p. 16.

[15] Reinhold Niebuhr, *The Nature and Destiny of Man* (New York: Charles Scribner's Sons, 1964), vol. 1, p. 140.

[16] Jean-Paul Sartre, *Existentialism and Human Emotions* (New York: Philosophical Library, 1957), p. 63.

[17] Susan Neiman, *Evil in Modern Thought* (Princeton, N.J.: Princeton University Press, 2002), p. 62.

11

THE CRUCIFIED GOD

THE BRIDGE OF SAN LUIS REY

Thornton Wilder wrote a novel about a rope bridge that broke and killed five people crossing it.

"On Friday noon, July the twentieth, 1714, the finest bridge in all Peru broke and precipitated five travelers into the gulf below. This bridge was on the high road between Lima and Cuzco and hundreds of persons passed over it every day. It had been woven of osier by the Incas more than a century before and visitors to the city were always led out to see it. It was a mere ladder of thin slats swung out over the gorge, with handrails of dried vine. Horses and coaches and

The cross alone truly justifies God.

chairs had to go down hundreds of feet below and pass over the narrow torrents on rafts, but no one, not even the Viceroy, not even the Archbishop of Lima, had descended with the baggage rather than cross by the famous bridge of San Luis Rey. . . . The bridge seemed to be among the things that last forever; it was unthinkable that it should break."[1]

The rest of the story centers on a Franciscan priest, Brother Juniper, who—convinced that nothing in God's universe happened by accident—determined to study the lives of the five in order to show the providence and wisdom of God even amid such a tragedy.

> **Brother Juniper was doing what theologians for centuries have done— trying to show the justice and goodness of God despite evil and suffering.**

"It seemed to Brother Juniper that it was high time for theology to take its place among the exact sciences and he long intended putting it there."[2]

Brother Juniper was doing what theologians for centuries have done—trying to show the justice and goodness of God despite evil and suffering. To borrow the words from Alexander Pope, he was seeking to "vindicate the ways of God to men"[3] or (from John Milton) to "assert Eternal Providence,/And justify the ways of God to man."[4] Scripture, too, touches on the theme, such as when David asks the Lord for forgiveness in order "that You may be found just when You speak, and blameless when You judge" (Psalm 51:4).

The question of God's goodness in a world reeking with pain and suffering remains difficult. Yet an answer exists, and it's found at only one place: the cross (Jesus' death). Any attempt to justify the ways of God apart from the cross—apart from a crucified God—is doomed.

THE PROBLEM OF PAIN

In her poem "In the Next Galaxy," Ruth Stone wrote:
"Things will be different.
No one will lose their sight,
their hearing, their gallbladder . . .
The idea of Hitler will not
have vibrated yet.
While back here,
they are still cleaning out
pockets of wrinkled
Nazis hiding in Argentina."[5]

Her words express the hope that some-where, sometime, life will be better than it is now, on a planet on which the "idea of Hitler" has long been vibrating. The hope of better things is tied to the question that we have been looking at: *How did things get bad to begin with?* How did "the idea of

PUBLIC DOMAIN

Adolf Hitler

Hitler," and everything else evil, arise in a world created by a loving God?

The attempt to answer that question is called *theodicy*, a theological term meaning "the justification of God" in the face of evil.

"The problem of suffering," Walter Kaufmann said, "is of crucial importance because it shows that the God of popular theism does not exist."[6]

Theodicy's an attempt to explain the goodness, power, and love of God *despite* human suffering. And that's we're doing.

And what have we so far seen?

First, that God had no choice

> If He wanted beings who could love Him, He had to make them free, and freedom means the capacity to choose wrong. Without that ability, there would be no freedom, and no freedom means no love.

at the very beginning of the problem. If He wanted beings who could love Him, He had to make them free, and freedom means the capacity to choose wrong. Without that ability, there would be no freedom, and no freedom means no love.

Thus love demands freedom, and so in order for humans to love they had to be free. But what demands human beings? The universe existed for billions of years without us. Nothing required our existence, certainly not the way love requires freedom.

THE RISK GOD TOOK

What this means, then, is that even though there's no *logical* reason we had to exist, God created us anyway, and He did so, knowing beforehand that each of us could possibly suffer, get sick, and die. That is, He created humanity realizing that it could fall and that if it did, evil would result.

Why would He do that?

The answer must be that, when all is over, a greater good will come out of this horrible experience of sin, suffering, and death. If God is all-loving and all-knowing, He must have created humanity knowing that even if it fell, a greater good would arise, and that ultimately it would be shown that He was just and fair and merciful in all His dealings with Lucifer, sin, evil, and us. If the questions of evil, justice, and sin are universal—involving intelligent life beyond our planet—then we have to believe that God will be exonerated and that His goodness, mercy, love, and justice will be vindicated in ways not readily apparent to us (because of our very limited view of reality) now. How could an all-loving God do any differently?

This idea of a greater good, of God being vindicated, leads, though, to what's perhaps the most troubling of all questions.

Why should an omnipotent, omniscient God be safely ensconced somewhere in the sky while, knowing the end from the beginning, He watches us fools crawl on our helpless bellies ignorant of even the next moment, much less the conclusion of all things?

As someone once asked: "If there is a greater good, if all of God's ways are to be exonerated in a grand and final harmony that vindicates God and all that has happened on earth, how can God justify working it out here, in the dirt, in human blood, sweat, and tears . . . while He sits enthroned in the glory of heaven? Whatever the profound questions, whatever the grand moral issues resolved in this struggle between good and evil, however efficiently and permanently the promised answers erase all doubts, iron out all absurdities, and wipe away all tears, the question remains: Why should an omnipotent, omniscient God be safely ensconced somewhere in the sky while, knowing the end from the beginning, He watches us fools crawl on our helpless bellies ignorant of even the next moment, much less the conclusion of all things? Why couldn't whatever point this all-loving God wanted to make be made by Him Himself, rather than with us human beings so miserably and inextricably drawn in through no choice of our own?"[7]

Good questions, and only one thing can answer them.

THE CRUCIFIED GOD

"*Never will it be forgotten that He whose power created and upheld the unnumbered worlds through the vast realms of space, the Beloved of God, the Majesty of heaven, He whom cherub and shining seraph delighted to adore—humbled Himself to uplift fallen man; that He bore the guilt and shame of sin, and the hiding of His Father's face, till the woes of a lost world broke His heart, and crushed out His life on Calvary's cross. That the Maker of all worlds, the Arbiter of all destinies, should lay aside his glory, and humiliate Himself from love to man, will ever excite the wonder and adoration of the universe.*"[8]

Christ Carrying the Cross, as portrayed by El Greco (Domenikos Theotokopoulos), c. 1580.

What's being depicted here? That Jesus Christ, even though the Creator of the universe— the one who not only created humans but made them with *free will*—had all the "woes of a lost world" fall on Him at once as He hung on the cross.

The cross, and it alone, answers the question about the justice and

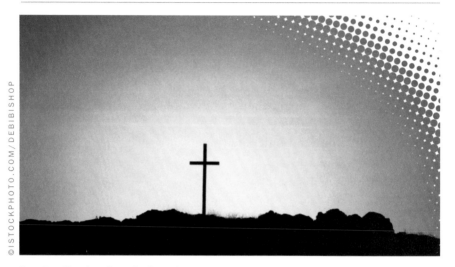

Any theodicy that doesn't place the cross at its center is doomed to choke on its own absurdities.

fairness of God amid suffering. Any theodicy that doesn't place the cross at its center is doomed to choke on its own absurdities. Only as we grasp the reality of God, the Creator, suffering in a way that no fallen human being has ever experienced can we begin to get some understanding of His goodness amid an evil world, a world in which we struggle with what Virgil called "the burdens of mortality." Far from being "safely ensconced somewhere in the sky," our Creator became one of us and suffered the results of sin in ways that no other human ever could. Only when we recognize that amazing truth can we begin to see hope beyond the fumes of a decaying race that rots even before its own corpses do.

And, fascinatingly enough, the clearest expression of God's suffering appears not in the New Testament but in the Old.

ISAIAH 53

"Who has believed our message and to whom has the arm of the Lord been revealed? He grew up before him like a tender shoot, and like a root out of dry ground. He had no beauty or majesty to attract us to him, nothing in his appearance that we should desire him. He was despised and rejected by men, a man of sorrows, and familiar with suffering. Like one from whom men hide their faces he was despised, and we esteemed him not. Surely he took up our infirmities and carried our sorrows, yet we considered him stricken by God, smitten by him, and afflicted. But he was pierced for our transgressions, he was crushed for our iniquities; the punishment that brought us peace was upon him, and by his wounds we are healed. We all, like sheep, have gone astray, each of us has turned to his own way; and the Lord has laid on him the iniquity of us all" (Isaiah 53:1-6, NIV).

The One suffering here is Jesus, and He is God the Creator—He who spun those billions of galaxies across the cosmos, and He who sustains them by "his powerful word" (Hebrews 1:3, NIV). Those texts are talking about God, in human flesh, suffering what no one else ever could.

People had been crucified before, of course, but that's not the focus of Christ's sufferings. Rather it involves substitution, of Him suffering for what others have done: "Surely *he took up our infirmities and carried our sorrows*, yet we considered him stricken by God, smitten by him, and afflicted. But he *was pierced for our transgressions, he was crushed for our iniquities; the punishment that brought us peace was upon him*, and by his wounds we are healed. We all, like sheep, have gone astray, each of us has turned to his own way; *and the Lord has laid on him the iniquity of us all*" (Isaiah 53:4-6, NIV).

> Far from being "safely ensconced somewhere in the sky," our Creator became one of us and suffered the results of sin in ways that no other human ever could.

Jesus "took up our infirmities and carried our sorrows" (verse 4). The Hebrew word translated "infirmities" (*holi*) has the connotations of "sickness, disease," while the word rendered "sorrow" (*makov*) represents "pain, physical pain, mental pain." Whose pain, whose sickness, whose disease, and whose woe did He bear at the cross? The whole world's! Christ died for each person. He bore the penalty for every sinner—and because we all are sinners, this means that He received the penalty for every human being.

But Scripture says even more. According to the text, He simultaneously bore all human suffering in Himself ("Surely he took up our infirmities and carried our sorrows"). What we suffer only as individuals—our own pain, sickness, and woe—He carried all Himself.

OTHER PEOPLE'S PAIN

Consider this idea: "My external sensations are no less private to myself than are my thoughts or my feelings. In either case my experience falls within my own circle, a circle closed on the outside."[9]

Pain is personal, more private than thought (you can share thought but not your pain), and so not one of the billions in the world's cauldron of disease and death ever suffered more than what each one, individually, could. Thus pain never goes beyond our "own circle, a circle closed on the outside." You can't feel anyone else's pain, and no one else can experience yours.

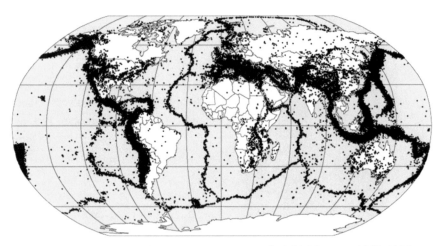

Preliminary Determination of Earthquake Epicenters (358,214 Events), 1963-1998. All the suffering from earthquakes and every other tragedy cannot equal what Christ went through on the cross.

"Human nature," Johann Goethe reminded us, "has its limitation. It can bear joy and suffering, and pain to a certain degree, but perishes when this point is passed."[10]

The sheer numbers of tragedy (125,000 in this tsunami, 100,000 in that earthquake, 2 million in this war, 500,000 in that one) stun us, but whether one or 1 million, each victim's pain was always and only his or her own, as if he or she suffered and died by himself or herself. In the whole wretched history of our whole wretched world, not one person ever suffered more than what only an individual could experience, no matter how many people might have been suffering together at once. Holocaust, famine, pandemic—it doesn't matter. Pain always comes in individual packets only.

> In the whole wretched history of our whole wretched world, not one person ever suffered more than what only an individual could experience. Except one time.

Except one time.

At the cross the woes of a lost and fallen world (its sickness, disease, pain, and suffering) all fell on Jesus *at once*. "Surely he took up our infirmities and carried our sorrows." That's the infirmities and sorrows of every human being who has ever lived or ever will. It was all there, concentrated at once onto the person of Jesus, God Himself, which means that God Himself has suffered from all of the free choice He gave us as human beings.

Who, then, can accuse God of indifference to, or of being distant from, our pain when He knows it more acutely than any of us, because He has experienced it more than all of us?

Albert Camus (of all people!) wrote: "Christ came to solve two problems, evil and death, which are precisely the problems that preoccupy the rebel. His solution consisted, first, in experiencing them.

The man-god suffers, too—with patience. Evil and death can no longer be entirely imputed to Him since He suffers and dies."[11]

Camus got it almost right. "Since He suffers and dies *worse than any human being could ever suffer or die*" would have been the better answer.

THEODICY

What have we seen?

If He wanted humans to be able to love, God had no choice except to create them free. But He didn't have to create them. Yet He did anyway, knowing all the possible suffering that could follow. However, because He's a loving God, He would, even knowing that these things might happen, nevertheless bring out a greater good, one that could make up for or justify all that came before. Even if so, how fair would it be that God would remain up in heaven, working out all these things for "a greater good," while we poor fools suffer and die down here in a cesspool of war, poverty, disease, and woe? It wouldn't be fair at all—which is why that's not what happened. Instead of staying in heaven, God Himself came down and entered the human race, and in our humanity suffered and died worse than any of the earth's billions ever had or ever could. In the end, when all's said and done, no one could justly point a finger at God in the sky and accuse Him of judging unfairly or of not understanding our pain when in reality

> In the end, when all's said and done, no one could justly point a finger at God in the sky and accuse Him of judging unfairly or of not understanding our pain when in reality He knew more pain than any human ever could.

He knew more pain than any human ever could. He experienced the pain of all humanity, something that no one else among the earth's wretched billions ever could know. God has united Himself to us in bonds of pain that He, and He alone, could have experienced.

Much still doesn't make sense about pain and suffering (but then, for example, much doesn't make sense about the nature of subatomic particles), yet that doesn't mean that God isn't there, or real, or that the promises of salvation, redemption, and eternal life aren't real either. On this side of eternity we'll never have all our questions answered about the seemingly mindless and meaningless flow of pain and woe. But what we do have is the reality of the cross and the fact that no human being has ever suffered or could ever suffer more than what God did.

And though that might not ease the pain we're going through now, it can at least offer us the hope that it's not all for nothing. Beyond that, it can help us set our own pain in the larger context of the struggle between good and evil. And it can enable us to cling to faith until we see fulfilled the promise: "God will wipe away every tear from their eyes; there shall be no more death, nor sorrow, nor crying. There shall be no more pain, for the former things have passed away" (Revelation 21:4).

[1] Thornton Wilder, *The Bridge of San Luis Rey* (New York: Harper and Row, 1998), p. 5.

[2] *Ibid.*, p. 7.

[3] Alexander Pope, *Essay on Man and Other Poems* (Mineola, N.Y.: Dover Publications, 1994), p. 46.

[4] John Milton, *Paradise Lost,* p. 9.

[5] Ruth Stone, *In the Next Galaxy* (Port Townsend, Wash.: Copper Canyon Press, 2004), p. 8.

[6] Walter Kaufmann, *The Faith of a Heretic* (New York: Doubleday Books, 1963), p. 137.

[7] Clifford Goldstein, *God, Gödel, and Grace: A Philosophy of Faith* (Hagerstown, Md.: Review and Herald Pub. Assn., 2003). pp. 50, 51.

[8] Ellen G. White, *The Great Controversy* (Mountain View, Calif.: Pacific Press Pub. Assn., 1911), p. 651. (Italics supplied.)

[9] F. H, Bradley, in T. S. Eliot, "The Waste Land," *The Complete Poems and Plays,* p. 54.

[10] Johann Wolfganf von Goethe, *The Sorrows of Young Werther* (New York: Signet Classics, 1962), p. 59.

[11] Albert Camus, *The Rebel: An Essay on Man in Revolt,* trans. Anthony Bower (New York: Alfred A. Knopf, 1956), p. 32.

SPOOKY ACTION AT A DISTANCE

MISS HARRIET

French author Guy de Maupassant wrote a story about a lonely God-fearing spinster named Miss Harriet whose passion, besides God, was art and nature. She meets a young rogue artist with whom she starts falling in love. When he doesn't reciprocate, Harriet, despondent, commits suicide by throwing herself down a well. The young artist, suffering from guilt, muses over her death: "I recognized, also, that she believed in a God, and that she hoped for compensation from him for the miseries she had endured. She had now

©PHOTODISC

Modern physics has shown that merely looking at one subatomic particle will affect another. It's as if glancing at one spinning billiard ball in Houston, Texas, will reverse the spin of another in Paris.

begun to decompose, and to become, in turn, a plant. She who had blossomed in the sun was now to be eaten up by cattle, carried away in herbs, and in the flesh of beasts, again to become human flesh. But that which is called the soul had been extinguished at the bottom of the dark well."[1]

Interesting thoughts . . . after all, what good did Miss Harriet's faith do her if, in the end, she wound up eaten by cattle, or incorporated into herbs?

Even with an understanding of the cross, and all the promises that have arisen from it, we come back to the kind of questions we raised earlier: "But what do these promises mean if Christians, those who follow Jesus, die just as everyone else does, and if at death all return to dust? From what we see now, there's no difference. The godliest saint's just as dead as the ungodliest sinner. How do we, then, understand the promises of salvation, redemption, and eternal life?"

Sure, it's helpful to understand that Christ on the cross suffered worse than any of us ever could. And sure, it's wonderful to believe that He died as a substitute for our sins. But Jesus rose from the grave, and the rest of the dead haven't. They're smack-dab left where we've dumped them, and if the past's a precursor to the future, we'll remain where others will dump us too.

All this even after Jesus, the Creator, suffered on the cross as a substitute for our sins?

What gives?

It's because all that we've looked at so far has dealt only with Christ's first coming—and the first coming, as we'll see, means little apart from what Scripture tells us will be His second.

SEASONS IN THE SUN

Poet Steve Gehrke writes about a childless woman who, "after the tumors started hatching in her chest," brought home 12 little fish, which she promptly dissected. Gehrke entertains the possibility of her stringing their hearts into a necklace and making earrings with their eyes ("when animals die, they pass into us"), and then reveals that this is what *she* wants: to have her flesh eaten— "to be digested, her blood washing through another heart."[2]

However macabre, Gehrke's poem reveals the human desire for immortality, the craving to keep on going (one way or another), the longing to find meaning and purpose in what otherwise seems so meaningless and purposeless.

Just ask Edna St. Vincent Millay:

"Not only under ground are the brains of men
Eaten by maggots.
Life in itself
Is nothing.
An empty cup, a flight of uncarpeted stairs.
Is it not enough that yearly, down this hill,
April
Comes like an idiot, babbling
and strewing flowers."[3]

Edna wasn't the only poet stressed out by April. Here's T. S. Eliot's spin on the month: "April is the cruelest month, breeding/Lilacs out of the dead land, mixing/Memory and desire, stirring/Dull roots with spring rain."[4]

With its stirring memories and blooming flowers, April mocks us with all those colorful explosions of life that, like us, are so fleeting. Like us, they will die, except that—unlike the buds and blooms—we know it. We're going to have our seasons in the sun, and then the maggots will eat the very brains we know it with, the same brains that tell us that the number of Aprils that budded and bloomed before us are few com-

> The human desire is for immortality, the craving to keep on going (one way or another), the longing to find meaning and purpose in what otherwise seems so meaningless and purposeless.

pared to all those that will come after, above, and without us. They will continue long after the names on our gravestones have weathered away, maybe even long after the gravestones themselves have disintegrated into the same atomic structures that we will have had already long decayed into. Both we and our gravestones all devolve to the same state. We just beat them to it, that's all. And if that's the case, it's hard to find meaning in anything we do.

> What has the cross changed? People still die and still rot in the ground, just as they did before Christ's arrival. Where is the hope of eternal life when even Christians wind up just as dead as non-Christians?

"Must I again declare to you," wrote Miguel de Unamuno, "the supreme vacuity of culture, of science, of art, of good, of truth, of beauty, of justice . . . of all these beautiful conceptions, if at the last, in four days or in four millions of centuries—it matters not which—no human consciousness shall exist to appropriate this civilization, this science, art, good, truth, beauty, justice, and all the rest?"[5]

Scripture, though, gives us another alternative—eternal life, a promise made certain through Jesus and His death on the cross.

THE SECOND COMING

Yet, one might rightly ask, what has the cross changed? People still die and still rot in the ground, just as they did before Christ's arrival. Where is the hope of eternal life when even Christians wind up just as dead as non-Christians?

The second coming of Jesus, that's where this hope is. Without the second, Christ wasted His time at the first. At His second coming the promises made at the first will finally and eternally reach fruition.

No wonder, then, that in Scripture the Second Coming plays such an important role and why so many texts refer to it. Here are just a few:

BIBLICAL PROMISES OF THE SECOND COMING

- "Let not your heart be troubled; you believe in God, believe also in Me. In My Father's house are many mansions; if it were not so, I would have told you. I go to prepare a place for you. And if I go and prepare a place for you, I will come again and receive you to Myself; that where I am, there you may be also" (John 14:1-3).

- "And as it is appointed for men to die once, but after this the judgment, so Christ was offered once to bear the sins of many. To those who eagerly wait for Him He will appear a second time, apart from sin, for salvation" (Hebrews 9:27, 28).

- "For the grace of God that brings salvation has appeared to all men, teaching us that, denying ungodliness and worldly lusts, we should live soberly, righteously, and godly in the present age, looking for the blessed hope and glorious appearing of our great God and Savior Jesus Christ" (Titus 2:11-13).

- "But of that day and hour no one knows, not even the angels of heaven, but My Father only. But as the days of Noah were, so also will the coming of the Son of Man be. For as in the days before the flood, they were eating and drinking, marrying and giving in marriage, until the day that Noah entered the ark, and did not know until the flood came and took them all away, so also will the coming of the Son of Man be" (Matthew 24:36-39).

- "Then the sign of the Son of Man will appear in heaven, and then all the tribes of the earth will mourn, and they will see the Son of Man coming on the clouds of heaven with power and great glory. And He will send His angels with a great sound of a trumpet, and they will gather together His elect from the four winds, from one end of heaven to the other" (Matthew 24:30, 31).

After His resurrection Jesus met with His followers. "Now when he had spoken these things, while they watched, He was taken up, and a cloud received Him out of their sight. And while they looked steadfastly toward heaven as He went up, behold, two men stood by them in white apparel, who also said, 'Men of Galilee, why do you stand gazing up into heaven? This same Jesus, who was taken up from you into heaven, will so come in like manner as you saw Him go into heaven'" (Acts 1:9-11).

Without question the Bible speaks about the second advent of Jesus. But what about the Second Coming makes it so important? What happens when Jesus returns that will solve the problem of death? How does the Second Coming bring to fruition what Christ did for us at His first appearing?

RESURRECTION

One of the most interesting (though hardly obvious) discoveries about human life is the bioelectrical aspect of our being. Whatever human life is, it's at least part electrical in nature. Like a lightbulb, without juice we're dead. Our nervous system is a bioelectrical grid that transmits signals throughout the body. Though not quite supercharged, we're charged nonetheless.

While hardly news to us today, this idea seemed remarkable when scientists first discovered it. Fascinated with the notion, a doctor in the 1800s—wanting a corpse for an experiment—offered a condemned convict cash to buy gin, beer, and beef before his hanging. The researcher's idea was simple: If electricity is the life force, could he not use it to revive a dead person?

Like a lightbulb, without juice we're dead.

The two made a deal. The man got his gin and beef; the doctor his corpse, to which he connected electric wires. After he threw the switch, the body (depending on where the wires were attached) kicked, twisted, contorted, genuflected, even smiled—everything but come back to life.

A few centuries later we have cryonics, which stores corpses in vats cooled with liquid nitrogen (about −320°F [−196°C]) in the hope that in 50, 500, or even 5,000 years they, thanks to scientific wonders, can be thawed out and brought back to life. Sometimes the whole body's preserved; other times just the head (the idea being that because consciousness resides in the brain, you'd still be you regardless of any new body attached below).

If that all sounds desperate, it is, reflecting how frantically humans want to beat death, our incorrigible foe, and just how fruitless all our efforts have been and always will be. And if we don't conquer death, then one day we're gone, along with everyone who ever remembered us.

And that's precisely why, according to the Bible, Jesus came to our world—to accomplish for us what we have never been able to do: once and forever defeat death and give life the meaning and purpose it was originally meant to have.

> **Jesus came to our world to accomplish for us what we have never been able to do: once and forever defeat death and give life the meaning and purpose it was originally meant to have.**

"Since the children have flesh and blood, he too shared in their humanity so that by his death he might destroy him who holds the power of death—that is, the devil" (Hebrews 2:14, NIV). "For the perishable must clothe itself with the imperishable, and the mortal with immortality. When the perishable has been clothed with the imperishable, and the mortal with immortality, then the saying that is written will come true: 'Death has been swallowed up in victory'" (1 Corinthians 15:53, 54, NIV).

But again, with the dead still in the ground, what do such passages mean? They're talking about the second coming of Jesus, when He raises the dead.

BIBLICAL PROMISES OF RESURRECTION

- "We will not all sleep, but we will all be changed—in a flash, in the twinkling of an eye, at the last trumpet. For the trumpet will sound, the dead will be raised imperishable, and we will be changed. For the perishable must clothe itself with the imperishable, and the mortal with immortality" (1 Corinthians 15:51-53, NIV).

- "For the Lord Himself will descend from heaven with a shout, with the voice of an archangel, and with the trumpet of God. And the dead in Christ will rise first. Then we who are alive and remain shall be caught up together with them in the clouds to meet the Lord in the air. And thus we shall always be with the Lord" (1 Thessalonians 4:16, 17).

- "Then the sign of the Son of Man will appear in heaven, and then all the tribes of the earth will mourn, and they will see the Son of Man coming on the clouds of heaven with power and great glory. And He will send His angels with a great sound of a trumpet, and they will gather together His elect from the four winds, from one end of heaven to the other" (Matthew 24:30, 31).

- "This is the will of the Father who sent Me, that of all He has given Me I should lose nothing, but should raise it up at the last day. And this is the will of Him who sent Me, that everyone who sees the Son and believes in Him may have everlasting life: and I will raise him up at the last day" (John 6:39, 40).

- "No one can come to Me unless the Father who sent Me draws him: and I will raise him up at the last day" (verse 44).

- "Do not marvel at this; for the hour is coming in the which all who are in the graves will hear His voice and come forth—those who have done good, to the resurrection of life" (John 5:28, 29).

- "I am the resurrection and the life. He who believes in Me, though he may die, he shall live" (John 11:25).

- "But now Christ is risen from the dead, and has become the firstfruits of those who have fallen asleep. For since by man came death, by Man also came the resurrection of the dead. For as in Adam all die, even so in Christ all shall be made alive. But each one in his own order: Christ the firstfruits, afterward those who are Christ's at His coming" (1 Corinthians 15:20-23).

The resurrection of the dead isn't just a hope—it is *the* hope, the thing that makes all that came before it real. The Second Coming is the climax and fruition of all that has gone before. Jesus will resurrect the dead, finally fulfilling all the wonderful promises about eternal life in Christ. Anything short of that leaves us with nothing but superstitions and lies. Only at the Second Coming, only when the graves open, will life itself be vindicated and shown not to be the absurdity and purposeless thing that it would have been if the graves had remained closed.

At Christ's return, in defiance of the world's wisdom, Jesus will appear in the sky, and with the same voice that summoned light and life into existence He will speak again. Then, through the power of His Word, the dead— whether now in magnificent stone tombs or in the bellies of worms— will rise and be reconstructed in bodies far surpassing anything human beings ever possessed, with the exception of Adam and Eve before the Fall. That's His ultimate promise—and it's the one promise that gives all the others any meaning at all.

> At Christ's return the dead will rise and be reconstructed in bodies far surpassing anything human beings ever possessed. That's His ultimate promise—and it's the one promise that gives all the others any meaning at all.

Spooky Action at a Distance

In the late 1800s a young gifted student from Germany wanted to study physics in college. His professors, who assured him that all the great breakthroughs in physics had already been made and that there was nothing else to learn, tried to discourage him from entering the field. Well, he went ahead and studied it anyway, and in a few years the young Max Planck became the founder of quantum theory, the most profound scientific revolution since Isaac Newton discovered gravity a few centuries earlier. Thanks to quantum physics we have such things as radios, television, computers, and lasers.

Yet the world of quantum physics is so weird, so bizarre, that our commonsense notions of cause and effect and how the world works become completely useless.

For example, when a subatomic explosion creates two particles, they fly away from each other. Each particle has a spin in one direction or the other. Physicists have proved that merely looking—yes, *looking*—at the spin of one particle causes the spin of the other to reverse itself even if it were a thousand or a million miles away. It's as if there are two spinning billiard balls, one in Paris and one in Houston, and your glance at the ball in Houston will cause the cue ball in Paris to whirl in the opposite direction.

How could that be? How could studying one particle affect another one miles away? And even

Max Planck presents Albert Einstein with the Max Planck medal of the German Physical Society, June 28, 1929, in Berlin.

more amazing, how can this change occur at a rate faster than the speed of light, something that really upset Einstein, who taught that information cannot move faster than light. Well, in the quantum world it does, which is why Einstein labeled the phenomenon "spooky action at a distance" and struggled with it his whole professional life.

What all this should tell us is that if the natural world can hold such deep mysteries, things that we can't rationally fathom, who should be surprised that we don't understand everything about the spiritual world, including the resurrection of the dead? And yet, all that being said, not even the resurrection of the dead is as hard to understand as quantum theory.

Christianity does not limit reality to the narrow and parochial worldview of equations, formulas, and theories. Whether feeding

5,000 with food meant for one (Matthew 14:15-21), or telling Peter to "go to the lake and throw out your line," then "take the fish you catch; open its mouth and you will find a four-drachma coin" "for my tax and yours" (Matthew 17:27, NIV), or raising a decaying corpse from the grave (John 11), Jesus revealed to us realms of reality in which science is too crude and clumsy to enter. By such acts He showed that limiting our worldview to what science alone tells us makes about as much sense as wearing bifocals to bed in hopes of seeing your dreams better. The Word of God presents reality as something broader, deeper, and grander than where equations, formulas, and theories can take us. But, again, nothing we're asked to believe by faith is as hard to grasp, logically, as is quantum theory.

Consider the implications of the following facts. According to the U.S. Bureau of the Census, the total population of the world (as projected for February 22, 2006, at 16:09 GMT) was about 6.5 billion. Add to this the 1,000 billion stars in our own galaxy. Astronomers estimate that the universe has at least 400 billion galaxies, each one flush with billions of stars.

POWER TO RAISE THE DEAD

Now (as Scripture says), if Jesus created all these things and upholds them with His own power, then couldn't He have the power to raise the dead, whose number is almost incomparably tiny in contrast to the number of stars He created?

Sure, the existence of hundreds of billions of galaxies

> Christianity does not limit reality to the narrow and parochial worldview of equations, formulas, and theories.

doesn't prove that the dead will be raised. What it does demonstrate is that an incredible power was involved in the creation of all of what exists. And if this power could originate everything that is (something far beyond what our minds can grasp), then why is it unreasonable to think that He could return some of the earth's dead to life (something far beyond what we can grasp as well)?

The power that could create and sustain billions of galaxies surely could re-create and bring back to life our dead, if He so chose. And that's exactly what the Bible says that He will do. If He doesn't, then everything about Jesus and the promises in the Word are all false.

The apostle Paul says as much. Talking to those who questioned, even denied, the physical bodily resurrection of the dead, he wrote: "But if it is preached that Christ has been raised from the dead, how can some of you say that there is no resurrection of the dead? If there is no resurrection of the dead, then not even Christ has been raised. And if Christ has not been raised, our preaching is useless and so is your faith. More than that, we are then found to be false witnesses about God, for we have testified about God that he raised Christ from the dead. But he did not raise him if in fact the dead are not raised. For if the dead are not raised, then Christ has not been raised either. And if Christ has not been raised, your faith is futile; you are still in your sins. Then those also who have fallen asleep in Christ are lost. If only for this life we have hope in Christ, we are to be pitied more than all men" (1 Corinthians 15:12-19, NIV).

> The power that could create and sustain billions of galaxies surely could re-create and bring back to life our dead, if He so chose. And that's exactly what the Bible says that He will do.

Paul closely ties the resurrection of Jesus with the final resurrection of the dead. And if no resurrection of the dead ever takes place, then it's all been futile. Those who have died are forever dead, and so will we eventually be, which means in the end it's all been for nothing.

That's what's at stake.

[1] Guy De Maupassant, *The Necklace and Other Short Stories* (Mineola, N.Y.: Dover Publications, 1992), p. 88.

[2] Steve Gehrke, "Because She Had No Children," *The Resurrection Machine* (Kansas City: BkMk Press, 2000), p. 17.

[3] Edna St. Vincent Millay, *First Fig and Other Poems* (Mineola, N.Y.: Dover Publications, 2000), p. 11.

[4] T. S. Eliot, "The Waste Land," *The Complete Poems and Plays,* p. 37.

[5] Miguel de Unamuno, *The Tragic Sense of Life* (Mineola, N.Y.: Dover Publications, 1954), p. 96.

KNOCKING ON HEAVEN'S DOOR?

BOOKMAKER OF VIRTUES

William J. Bennett had acquired the reputation as (sort of) the moral conscience of America. At least that was how he had packaged himself. And quite successfully too, going by book sales at least. For more than 20 years the former Reagan administration honcho was a frontline general in the "culture wars." Whether excoriating academic permissiveness on American college campuses, bemoaning Bill Clinton's office peccadilloes, lambasting homosexual

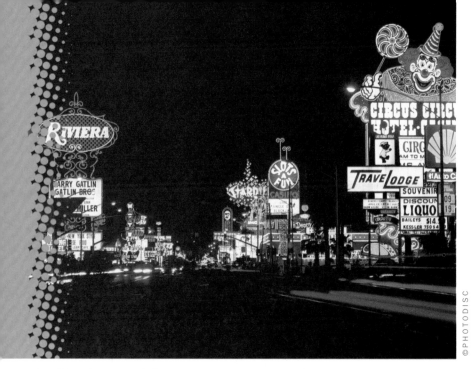

Gamblers throw away billions every year because the odds are always against them.

marriages or the "unrestricted personal liberty" that was destroying America's families, Bennett let it be known that the nation needed to repent and change its ways.

And he struck a chord, too. He must have, because he had been asking for, and getting, about $50,000 per speech—not a bad living, especially when you add to that the millions in royalties from his best-selling books on morality, such as *The Broken Hearth: Reversing the Moral Collapse of the American Family; The Book of Virtues;* and *The Death of Outrage.*

All this was fine, except for one problem. William Bennett had taken about $8 million of the money he made preaching about moral-ity—and lost it gambling!

"Bennett—who gambled throughout Clinton's impeachment—has continued this pattern in subsequent years. . . . For instance, Bennett lost $340,000 at Caesar's Boardwalk Regency in Atlantic City. And . . . he lost more than $500,000 at the Bellagio in Las Vegas. 'There's a term in the trade for this kind of gambler,' says a casino source who has witnessed Bennett at the high-limit slots in the wee hours. 'We call them losers.'"[1]

He's not alone, either. Gamblers threw away $68.7 billion at casinos, tracks, lottery outlets, legal sports books, bingo halls, charity gaming halls, and card rooms in the United States in 2006. That's just one year (and one country). The fact is, gamblers are always losers (the exceptions being so small that they don't count). Every casino everywhere exists only because people such as Bill Bennett (who checked himself into gambling detox after being outed) leave behind a lot more money there than they take home.

> Every casino everywhere exists only because people such as Bill Bennett (who checked himself into gambling detox after being outed) leave behind a lot more money there than they take home. The odds are always against you.

The odds are *always* against you. They have to be. If not, and enough people won, the gambling joints would disappear.

It's sad when people throw away fortunes, big and small, gambling against the odds. What's even sadder, though, is to throw away the promise of eternal life when the odds are dramatically in your favor of getting it. God presents us with something so good, with odds *so* in our favor, that we can't lose unless we choose to.

What are we talking about?

HISTORY LESSON

We ended the previous chapter discussing Jesus Christ and His promise of eternal life. With so much at stake in that promise (i.e., eternal life or eternal destruction) it's no wonder that God has given us good reasons to believe in it. And one of them appears in the second chapter of the Old Testament book of Daniel, which gives powerful and convincing evidence for us to trust in the promise of His coming and the eternity that it ushers in.

In fact, He gives us odds that only a fool would dare bet against!

The setting is the ancient Near East, about 600 years before Christ. As is the case even today, turmoil filled the region. It was basically just one war after another. In this case Babylon, the military behemoth of that time (occupying the territory of modern Iraq) trounced the tiny nation of Judah (where part of modern Israel is today) in a series of invasions that by 587 B.C. had left the little nation in ruins, with many of its upper class and royalty either dead or deported. This section of the Bible centers on four young men who were, early on, taken in captivity to Babylon itself.

"Now from among those of the sons of Judah were Daniel, Hananiah, Mishael, and Azariah. To them the chief of the eunuchs gave names: he gave Daniel the name Belteshazzar; to Hananiah, Shadrach; to Mishael, Meshach; and to Azariah, Abed-Nego" (Daniel 1:6, 7).

Having demonstrated superior knowledge and talent, they received special training in their captive nation and became part of an elite group serving in the king's court. The experiences they went through give us additional reasons to trust in the promise of the resurrection.

"Now in the second year of Nebuchadnezzar's reign, Nebuchadnezzar had dreams; and his spirit was so troubled that his sleep left him. Then the king gave the command to call the magicians, the astrologers, the sorcerers, and the Chaldeans to

Plan of the city of Babylon during the time of King Nebuchadnezzar II, 600 B.C.

PUBLIC DOMAIN

tell the king his dreams. So they came and stood before the king. And the king said to them, 'I have had a dream, and my spirit is anxious to know the dream.'

159

"Then the Chaldeans spoke to the king in Aramaic, 'O king, live forever! Tell your servants the dream, and we will give the interpretation.'

"The king answered and said to the Chaldeans, 'My decision is firm: if you do not make known the dream to me, and its interpretation, you shall be cut in pieces, and your houses shall be made an ash heap. However, if you tell the dream and its interpretation, you shall receive from me gifts, rewards, and great honor. Therefore tell me the dream and its interpretation.'

"They answered again and said, 'Let the king tell his servants the dream, and we will give its interpretation.'

"The king answered and said, 'I know for certain that you would gain time, because you see that my decision is firm: if you do not make known the dream to me, there is only one decree for you! For you have agreed to speak lying and corrupt words before me till the time has changed. Therefore tell me the dream, and I shall know that you can give me its interpretation.'

> "The king answered and said to the Chaldeans, 'My decision is firm: if you do not make known the dream to me, and its interpretation, you shall be cut in pieces.'"

"The Chaldeans answered the king, and said, 'There is not a man on earth who can tell the king's matter; therefore no king, lord, or ruler has ever asked such things of any magician, astrologer, or Chaldean. It is a difficult thing that the king requests, and there is no other who can tell it to the king except the gods, whose dwelling is not with flesh.'

"For this reason the king was angry and very furious, and gave a command to destroy all the wise men of Babylon. So the decree went out, and they began killing the wise men; and they sought Daniel and his companions, to kill them" (Daniel 2:1-13).

God sent Nebuchadnezzar a dream that outlined history.

As the story continues, Daniel not only recounts for the king the dream that the ruler couldn't remember, but then gives him the interpretation, thus saving everyone's life—including his own.

"You, O king, were watching; and behold, a great image! This great image, whose splendor was excellent, stood before you; and its form was awesome. This image's head was of fine gold, its chest and arms of silver, its belly and thighs of bronze, its legs of iron, its feet partly of iron and partly of clay. You watched while a stone was cut out without hands, which struck the image on its feet of iron and clay, and broke them to pieces. Then the iron, the clay, the bronze, the silver, and the gold were crushed together, and became like chaff from the summer threshing floors; the wind carried them away so that no trace of them was found. And the stone that struck the image became a great mountain and filled the whole earth.

"This is the dream. Now we will tell the interpretation of it before the king" (verses 31-36).

A Historic Dream

Thus the king dreams about a giant statue made of various metals. The head was of gold, the arms and chest of silver, the belly and thighs brass, the legs iron, the feet and toes a mixture of iron and clay. At the end of the dream a giant rock smashes the statue until nothing of it remains.

Then in the last half of Daniel 2 the prophet interprets the dream, explaining that the various metals symbolized empires that would rise and fall until the end of our present world.

"You, O king, are a king of kings. For the God of heaven has given you a kingdom, power, strength, and glory; and wherever the children of men dwell, or the beasts of the field and the birds of the heaven, He has given them into your hand, and has made you ruler over them all—you are this head of gold. But after you shall arise another kingdom inferior to yours; then another, a third kingdom of bronze, which shall rule over all the earth. And the fourth kingdom shall be strong as iron, inasmuch as iron breaks in pieces and shatters everything; and like iron that crushes, that kingdom will break in pieces and crush all the others. Whereas you saw the feet and toes, partly of potter's clay and partly of iron, the kingdom shall be divided; yet the strength of the iron shall be in it, just as you saw the iron mixed with ceramic clay. And as the toes of the feet were partly of iron and partly of clay, so the kingdom shall be partly strong and partly fragile. As you saw iron mixed with ceramic clay, they will mingle with the seed of men: but they will not adhere to one another, just as iron does not mix with clay. And in the days of these kings the God of heaven will

> Daniel interprets the dream, explaining that the various metals symbolized empires that would rise and fall until the end of our present world.

set up a kingdom which shall never be destroyed; and the kingdom shall not be left to other people; it shall break in pieces and consume all these kingdoms, and it shall stand forever. Inasmuch as you saw that the stone was cut out of the mountain without hands, and that it broke in pieces the iron, the bronze, the clay, the silver, and the gold—the great God has made known to the king what will come to pass after this. The dream is certain, and its interpretation is sure" (verses 37-45).

History shows that Babylon, the "head of gold" (verse 38), did, indeed, come and go, just as Daniel had predicted.

The second kingdom (the arms and chest of silver), Media Persia ("after you shall arise another kingdom inferior to yours" [verse 39]), arrived and went, as predicted.

The third kingdom, Greece ("a third kingdom of bronze, which shall rule over all the earth" [verse 39]), also made its appearance on the stage of history.

The fourth kingdom of iron legs, obviously the Roman Empire ("and the fourth kingdom shall be strong as iron" [verse 40]), rose and fell, again according to the prophecy.

Next, Daniel said that the fourth kingdom would not be replaced by another single empire. Instead it would fracture into lesser kingdoms, some stronger than others, and these kingdoms would never reunite, even through the connections of family and marriage. "Whereas you saw the feet and toes, partly of potter's clay

The image in Nebuchadnezzar's dream reveals a succession of empires eventually destroyed by God's own kingdom.

JAMES PADGETT

and partly of iron, the kingdom shall be divided. . . . And as the toes of the feet were partly of iron and partly of clay, so the kingdom shall be partly strong and partly fragile. As you saw iron mixed with ceramic clay, they will mingle with the seed of men; but they will not adhere to one another, even as iron does not mix with clay" (verses 41-43).

What better—and more accurate—prediction could anyone have made about the breakup of the Roman Empire into what ultimately has become the divided nations (some weak, some strong) of Europe and the other former Roman territory surrounding the Mediterranean Sea?

Notice, especially, that Daniel was talking about the mingling of seed—intermarriage obviously. For centuries royal dynasties and families married into each other to cement political alliances.

ROYAL CONNECTIONS

"A well-known example of royal intermarriage and interrelation today is that of Elizabeth II of the United Kingdom and Prince Philip, Duke of Edinburgh (born a Prince of Greece and Denmark). Prince Philip is the son of Prince Andrew of Greece and Denmark and

PUBLIC DOMAIN

Princess Alice of Battenberg, whose mother, Princess Victoria of Hesse and by Rhine, and paternal grandfather, Prince Alexander of Battenberg, were both members of the same paternal family. Princess Alice's father's brother, Prince Henry of Battenberg, meanwhile, married Princess Beatrice (a daughter of Elizabeth II's great-great-grandmother, Queen Victoria). Their daughter, Victoria Eugenie of Battenberg, married King Alfonso XIII of Spain, and her grandson, the present king, Juan Carlos, married Princess Sophia of Greece and

Queen Victoria and her daughter Princess Beatrice

Denmark, whose father was a cousin of Prince Philip, Duke of Edinburgh. Alternatively, Queen Elizabeth's great-great-grandfather, King Christian IX of Denmark, was also Prince Philip's great-grandfather. They are also related several times through Princess Sophia, Electress of Hanover."[2]

And yet even intermarriage could not reunite all the territories of the former Roman Empire. What did Daniel say would happen? "Whereas you saw the feet and the toes, partly of potter's clay and partly of iron, the kingdom shall be divided. . . . And as the toes of the feet were partly of iron and partly of clay, so the kingdom shall be partly strong and partly fragile. As you saw iron mixed with ceramic clay, they will mingle with the seed of men; but they will not adhere to one another, just as iron does not mix with clay" (verses 41-43). In other words, they would not reunify, despite an endless number of attempts to do just that!

> More than 26 centuries ago Daniel accurately depicted the rise and fall of the Roman Empire and the state of political affairs in its aftermath, even to today.

What an accurate depiction of the history of the former Roman territories, ranging from Europe around the eastern end of the Mediterranean Sea and across northern Africa. Since the collapse of the Roman Empire its former parts have constantly fought each other. In short, they have not adhered to one another, "just as iron does not mix with clay."

Which means that more than 26 centuries ago Daniel accurately depicted the rise and fall of the Roman Empire and the state of political affairs in its aftermath, even to today.

What's left? The giant rock that smashes all these kingdoms and leaves nothing behind. And that's God establishing His eternal kingdom, which is what happens after the Second Coming and God raises the righteous dead to eternal life. "And in the days of these kings the God of heaven will set up a kingdom which shall never be destroyed" (verse 44).

Odds-on Favorite

Look at the odds. Babylon, Media-Persia, Greece, pagan Rome, Europe, and the modern Mediterranean world—all came, in order, just as Daniel had predicted. The only kingdom left in the prophecy, and the only one that we, from our perspective, haven't yet seen fulfilled is the last, Christ's eternal kingdom, which He establishes after the resurrection of the dead.

Five out of the six steps leading to the promise of His coming have met their fulfillment. Daniel was right on the first five. Who could not trust him on the sixth? The odds are in his favor.

The evidence here is as broad, as real, as firm, and as factual as world history itself. The universe could collapse on itself tomorrow, but there will have always been a Babylon, a Media-Persia, a Greece, and a Rome that eventually broke up into the nations of modern Europe, North Africa, and the Middle East—just as Daniel had predicted. If there were a God who wanted to give us rational and logical evidence for His existence, what more firm foundation, what broader and immovable foundation, could He offer than world history itself?

Modern Mediterranean basin, the site of the ancient Roman Empire.

What other worldview presents a background able to explain Daniel 2? A secular, atheistic one that denies any kind of supernatural transcendence will reject what the chapter all but proves. What natural laws, what physical phenomenon, can explain how a man living 2,600 years ago could so accurately depict future events that he, of himself, could not possibly have known?

On the other hand, if there is a transcendent personal God who not only knows the future but is willing to reveal it to humans, then we have an answer. How else could Daniel, living centuries before some of these events, so accurately predict them?

> What natural laws, what physical phenomenon, can explain how a man living 2,600 years ago could so accurately depict future events that he, of himself, could not possibly have known?

God here doesn't seem to be merely the best explanation. Logically, rationally, He is the *only* explanation—and with it we have powerful evidence to trust Him about the last kingdom, the one established when Jesus returns at the Second Coming.

THE FIRST COMING

Finally, and most important, the greatest evidence for the Second Coming is the fact of the first. Again we find ourselves dealing with the question of what difference Christ's death has made when the dead are still dead. The best, the worst, the most sinful, the most saintly—all have utterly decomposed or are on the fast track there. Without the promised resurrection, what good did Christ's death do—for anyone?

Nothing. Paul says so: "For if the dead are not raised, then Christ has not been raised either. And if Christ has not been raised, your faith is futile; you are still in your sins" (1 Corinthians 15:16, 17, NIV).

So unless we're to believe that Christ's incarnation, life, death, and resurrection were for nothing, then the faithful dead have to rise to eternal life. Though Christ's first coming doesn't *prove* the reality of the second, at least in the sense of "scientific" proof (whatever that really means), His second coming and the resurrection of the dead is the ultimate and final vindicator of the first, the event that ultimately validates all that Christ did through His life and death.

KNOCKING ON HEAVEN'S DOOR?

Wait a minute. What about heaven? And hell? Don't the saved at death soar like a helium-filled balloon to heavenly bliss while the leaden lost plummet into the inferno of eternal torment? Isn't that standard Christian fare, the stuff of endless radio broadcasts and Sunday sermons? How does one reconcile the resurrection of the dead at the Second Coming with people going to heaven or hell immediately at death as if their last heartbeat spurted them in one direction or the other?

One doesn't. Despite vigorous and imaginative theological gymnastics that attempt to meld both positions into one coherent teaching, either the dead are, in general, asleep, unconscious and oblivious to everything, or they're in the bliss of heaven or (as the case may be) the torture of hell.

Which is correct?

Let's look at what Scripture has to say about death. Do the following passages make more sense if the

> Either the dead are, in general, asleep, unconscious and oblivious to everything, or they're in the bliss of heaven or the torture of hell.

©PHOTODISC

dead are asleep, awaiting the resurrection, or in heavenly bliss (or hellish torment)? That's the only question: in light of these texts, which position makes sense, and which is nonsensical?

WHAT DOES DEATH BRING?

The patriarch Job, after losing his possessions, his family, and his health, longed for death. What did he understand that death would bring?

"Why did I not perish at birth, and die as I came from the womb? Why were there knees to receive me and breasts that I might be nursed? For now I would be lying down in peace; I would be asleep and at rest with kings and counselors of the earth, who built for themselves places now lying in ruins, with rulers who had gold, who filled their houses with silver. Or why was I not hidden in the ground like a stillborn child, like an infant who never saw the light of day? There the wicked cease from turmoil, and there the weary are at rest. Captives also enjoy their ease; they no longer hear the slave driver's shout. The small and the great are there, and the slave is freed from his master" (Job 3:11-19, NIV).

Does this sound as if Job envisioned death as a conscious state, or as a sleep, a rest?

What about Jesus, who said: "Do not marvel at this; for the hour is coming in which all who are in the graves will hear His voice and come forth—those who have done good, to the resurrection of life, and those who have done evil, to the resurrection of condemnation" (John 5:28, 29)? Are the dead here asleep in the grave until the resurrection, or are they in heaven or hell?

"And many of those who sleep in the dust of the earth shall awake, some to everlasting life, some to shame and everlasting contempt" (Daniel 12:2). Which position, in light of this passage, makes sense? If the dead received their reward or punishment as soon as they died, what is the verse talking about?

Or this one? "For in death there is no remembrance of You; in the grave who will give You thanks?" (Psalm 6:5). Are the dead in the bliss of heaven (or torment of hell) or asleep in the grave? If the first, what is the text talking about?

In response to those who denied the resurrection of the dead, Paul wrote: "And if Christ is not risen, your faith is futile; you are still in your sins! Then also those who have fallen asleep in Christ have perished" (1 Corinthians 15:17, 18). *Those fallen asleep (the dead) in Christ are lost if there's no resurrection?* How could that be if the dead in Christ are already in heaven? If they are in heaven, the texts become nonsensical. But if they are unconscious in the grave, the texts make perfect sense.

WAITING FOR THEIR REWARD

Here's Jesus again, talking specifically about His second coming: "And behold, I am coming quickly, and My reward is with Me, to give to every one according to his work" (Revelation 22:12). He's bringing His reward with Him? Don't the faithful dead get it immediately at death, soaring off to heaven, at least as commonly taught? Many of Christ's faithful followers have been dead for centuries.

Certainly they should have been enjoying their reward long before now, much less whenever the Second Coming gets here. Yet that's not what Jesus states. The reward comes *with* Him. On the other hand, if His faithful followers are still dead, asleep and knowing nothing, the words make sense. Only when Jesus returns and raises them will they receive their reward.

The dead still wait in their graves for their reward.

Again, what do the following passages about death mean if, indeed, the deceased are in heaven or hell? "When their spirit departs, they return to the ground; on that very day their plans come to nothing" (Psalm 146:4, NIV). "The dead do not praise the Lord, nor any who go down into silence" (Psalm 115:17). "For the living know that they will die; but the dead know nothing" (Ecclesiastes 9:5).

Again, all these are difficult texts unless the dead are unconscious ("the dead know nothing") until the resurrection.

One of the most revealing stories in the Bible about death oc-curred when Lazarus, a friend of Christ, died. Upon hearing the news of his death, Jesus said: "'Our friend Lazarus sleeps, but I go that I may wake him up.' Then His disciples said, 'Lord, if he sleeps, he will get well.' However, Jesus spoke of his death, but they thought that he was speaking about taking rest in sleep. Then Jesus said to them plainly, 'Lazarus is dead'" (John 11:11-14).

> Jesus equated death with sleep, not with some conscious state of existence.

Jesus equated death with sleep, not with some conscious state of existence. In fact, dozens of times the Bible depicts death as a sleep.

What happened next with Lazarus?

As He approached Bethany, Jesus met Martha, Lazarus' sister, who told him that her brother had been dead for four days. Notice what Jesus told her: "'Your brother will rise again.' Martha said to Him, 'I know that he will rise again in the resurrection at the last day.' Jesus said to her, 'I am the resurrection and the life. He who believes in Me, though he may die, he shall live'" (verses 23, 24).

Again, which of the two positions makes better sense in light of the incident? In fact, which is the only rational one? Why would she be talking about her brother rising in the resurrection if he is already in heaven? And why would Jesus say to her that "he *shall* live" if Lazarus is already alive and enjoying his eternal reward? If, on the other hand, he is asleep, unconscious until he rises "in the resurrection of the last day," the whole dialogue is perfectly understandable.

> If Lazarus was in the bliss of heaven, why didn't Jesus say, "Lazarus, come down," instead of "Lazarus, come forth"?

"Then they took away the stone from the place where the dead man was lying. . . . Now when He [Jesus] had said these things, He cried with a loud voice, 'Lazarus, come forth!' And he who had died came out" (verses 41-43).

Now, if Lazarus was in the bliss of heaven, why didn't Jesus say, "Lazarus, come down," instead of "Lazarus, come forth"? Don't His words indicate that Lazarus was simply asleep in the tomb rather than in heaven? As with all the passages that we have looked at, it makes sense only if the dead are asleep, awaiting Christ's return, as opposed to immediate reward or punishment at death.

WITH JESUS IN PARADISE

OK, all this is fine. The "good" dead and the "bad" dead—in fact, all the dead (with a few notable exceptions)—are asleep, awaiting their final reward or punishment. It's hard to see—considering what we've just looked at—how it could be otherwise.

Yet, to be fair, what about passages that seem to teach immediate reward or punishment at death?

Fortunately, not too many exist, and a closer look—particularly at their context and in light of other clear biblical testimony—reveals that they're not teaching anything different about death than the previous texts.

The mostly commonly cited verse used to buttress the argument that the righteous immediately go off to heaven at death occurs in the book of Luke's account of the crucifixion of Christ with two thieves.

"Then one of the criminals who were hanged blasphemed Him, saying, 'If you are the Christ, save Yourself and us.' But the other, answering, rebuked him, saying, 'Do you not even fear God, seeing you are under the same condemnation? And we indeed justly, for we receive the due reward of our deeds; but this Man has done nothing wrong.' Then he said to Jesus, 'Lord, remember me when You come into Your kingdom.' And Jesus said unto him, 'Assuredly, I say to you, today you will be with Me in paradise'" (Luke 23:39-43).

The key verse is the last, which in a more modern version reads: "And He said to him, 'Truly I say to you, today you shall be with Me in Paradise'" (verse 43, NASB).

Is Jesus really telling the thief that he, the criminal, will be with Jesus in Paradise that very day? If so, then what about all those previous passages that unambiguously teach something else about death?

PUNCTUATION MAKES ALL THE DIFFERENCE

We find the answer in the punctuation. Notice how one simple punctuation adjustment radically alters the meaning of what Jesus said. Here are the same words of Jesus, *the words originally written down in the Greek manuscripts without punctuation* (punctuation marks were added centuries later), only now with a punctuation change: "Truly I say to you today, you shall be with Me in Paradise."

What's the difference? The text that had Jesus telling the criminal that he would be in Paradise that same day now has Jesus saying nothing of the sort. The comma, commonly placed *before* the word "today" ("Truly I say to you, today you shall . . ."), is now placed *after* it ("Truly I say to you today, you shall ...")—and the mean-

Jesus' statement to the dying thief on the cross has often been misunderstood.

HOWARD SANDEN

173

ing completely changes. Jesus wasn't notifying the thief where he would be immediately after death. The emphasis was to assure the dying man *at that moment*, as in "today," that he would have a place in Christ's kingdom. The sense of immediacy was on the assurance of salvation, not on what happens at death. *Truly I'm telling you*—today, right now—*that you will have salvation.*

Look at the context. The Roman authorities were executing two criminals, one repentant, one not, along with Jesus. The repentant one sees in Jesus the Savior and asks for salvation. Is He going to preach the thief a sermon on what happens at death, or is He going to give the thief what he needs at the moment of his great trial: the assurance of salvation? Though a common thief dying a criminal's death, he receives from Jesus, right at that moment, "today" (when he needs it, because soon he'll be dead), the promise of salvation.

Understood this way, the text fits in perfectly with all the others cited earlier. If we view Luke 23:43 as commonly understood, we're faced with the Bible contradicting itself in a big way.

> **Why would Jesus tell the thief that he would be in Paradise that day when Jesus Himself didn't even go there until later?**

Also, why would Jesus tell the thief that he would be in Paradise that day when Jesus Himself didn't even go there until later? Christ died on Friday, was in the tomb Saturday, and was resurrected on Sunday. When Mary appeared to Him on Sunday morning, what did He tell her? "Do not cling to Me, *for I have not yet ascended to My Father;* but go to My brethren and say to them, 'I am ascending to My Father and your Father; and to My God and your God'" (John 20:17).

What does He mean that He has not yet ascended to the Father or heaven, when two days earlier, on Friday, He supposedly told the thief that that day both would be there? If the comma (again, something inserted into the text centuries after its composition) remains before the word "today," then Jesus should have been in Paradise with the thief on Friday. Yet here He is, on Sunday morning, telling Mary that He has not yet ascended to the Father (as in "Our Father in heaven" [Matthew 6:9]). Again, how could that be when, on Friday, He told the thief that both of them, that day, would be in Paradise?

People in these ancient tombs will be restored to life only because Jesus rose from His tomb.

Once more the answer's simple: Jesus, along with the thief, rested in the tomb on Sabbath. On Sunday Jesus rose from the dead. Jesus and the thief weren't together in Paradise on Friday, and thus Luke 23:43 fits perfectly with all the others about the condition of the dead.

EARTHLY TENTS

Paul has several statements commonly misinterpreted to teach consciousness in death:

"Now we know that if the earthly tent we live in is destroyed, we have a building from God, an eternal house in heaven, not built by human hands. Meanwhile we groan, longing to be clothed with our heavenly dwelling, because when we are clothed, we will not be found naked. For while we are in this tent, we groan and are burdened, because we do not wish to be unclothed but to be clothed with our heavenly dwelling, so that what is mortal may be swallowed up by life. Now it is God who has made us for this very purpose and has given us the Spirit as a deposit, guaranteeing what is to come. Therefore we are always confident and know that as long as we are at home in the body we are away from the Lord. We live by faith, not by sight. We are confident, I say, and would prefer to be away from the body and at home with the Lord. So we make it our goal to please him, whether we are at home in the body or away from it. For we must all appear before the judgment seat of Christ, that each one may receive what is due him for the things done while in the body, whether good or bad" (2 Corinthians 5:1-10, NIV).

Paul's point here is simple: as human beings in this world, in this "earthly tent"—that is, our mortal bodies—we will suffer, groan, and be burdened. But, he declares, don't give up hope, because we have the promise of a "heavenly dwelling," the time when "what is mortal may be swallowed up by life," that is, *eternal life*. He contrasts the idea of being "home in the body" (existing in our mortals bodies here and now) with the promise of eternal life in Jesus, which he describes as being "at home with the Lord." Paul isn't saying that the moment you die, the moment you shed your "earthly dwelling," you'll be "at home with the Lord" in heaven. No, he's reminding us that for now we have earthly bodies (and thus we'd better behave while in them, because we will one day stand at the judgment seat), but the time is coming when we'll "be at home with the Lord" and shed our present "earthly dwelling." Thus, when Paul writes that "we are confident, I say, and would prefer to be away from the body and at home with the Lord," he is simply stating, *I'd rather be in heaven, with Jesus, than here in this world*. He's not talking about what happens immediately at death. How can he be, when he and other Bible writers are so clear that the dead sleep and remain that way until Christ returns?

Paul would rather be in heaven, with Jesus, than here in this world.

Another passage used to teach that the dead are in heaven also comes from Paul:

"For I know that through your prayers and the help given by the Spirit of Jesus Christ, what has happened to me will turn out for my deliverance. I eagerly expect and hope that I will in no way be ashamed, but will have sufficient courage so that now as always Christ will be exalted in my body, whether by life or by death. For to me, to live is Christ and to die is gain. If I am to go on living in the body, this will mean fruitful labor for me. Yet what shall I choose? I do not know! I am torn between the two: I desire to depart and be with Christ, which is better by far; but it is more necessary for you that I remain in the body. Convinced of this, I know that I will remain, and I will continue with all of you for your progress and joy in the faith, so that through my being with you again your joy in Christ Jesus will overflow on account of me" (Philippians 1:19-26, NIV).

> **As far as Paul is concerned, the moment he closes his eyes in death, whether Christ comes back in two minutes or 2,000 years, it will make no difference to him.**

Again, he is the same Paul who said that if there is no resurrection, then those who died in Christ are lost, which makes no sense if they at death go right to heaven with Jesus.

What, then, does Paul mean? Basically what he said in the passage from Corinthians: We live in this world, in this body, but we have the promise of a new life in Jesus. He's dealing with two states: this life, and that of life eternal "with Christ." The apostle would rather be in heaven "with Christ" than here. "I am torn between the two: I desire to depart and be with Christ, which is better by far; but it is more necessary for you that I remain in the body." Paul isn't claiming that as soon as he dies He'll be "with Christ," for he knows that the dead are asleep. Instead, as far as he is concerned, the moment he closes his eyes in death, whether Christ comes back in two minutes or 2,000 years, it will make no difference to him. He dies, and the next thing He knows he will "be with Christ," regardless of all the time that has passed.

But what about the time that Moses and Elijah appeared to Jesus and some of the disciples? "After six days Jesus took with him Peter,

James and John the brother of James, and led them up a high mountain by themselves. There he was transfigured before them. His face shone like the sun, and his clothes became as white as the light. Just then there appeared before them Moses and E lijah, talking with Jesus" (Matthew 17:1-3, NIV).

The incident would, for sure, refute the idea of the dead sleeping except that, according to the Bible, Elijah went to heaven *without* having even died (2 Kings 2:1, 11), and a text in the New Testament that, while not overtly clear, implies that Moses, having died, was resurrected (Jude 9). Thus one shouldn't be quick to draw, from one account of two unique men, a paradigm for all the dead, especially with the numerous other texts that teach death is a sleep.

NEAR-DEATH EXPERIENCES

Another argument used to support the idea of a conscious afterlife involves accounts of people who have claimed to have died, then, after coming back to life, give fantastic accounts of meeting spiritual beings, of seeing their beloved dead, and/or of talking with angels or even with a divine figure whom many associate with God or Jesus.

Many have had what they call "out of body" experiences in which they enter a tunnel of light.

For instance, consider the following:

"In front of me I saw a small light in the vast distance. The light started to get larger. It became more brilliant and it stopped in front of me. I felt an intense love, which came from the Light. I know without a doubt that this beautiful intense loving Light was God. The Light started to communicate with me; but the communication was telepathic, it was not verbal. The Light asked me if I wanted to come with it. At this point I completely understood the nature of the question and the consequences of my answer. If I chose to continue with the Light I knew that I would die and never return to earth. I thought about this and replied that I thought that I still had important things to do back there [on earth]. At that point the Light began to recede. I found myself waking up on the bed of my dorm room."[3]

Or this one:

"After suffering from a terminal illness, in 1982 Mellen-Thomas Benedict 'died' and for an hour and a half he was monitored showing no vital signs. Miraculously he returned to his body with a complete remission of the disease—and what may be the most inspirational near-death-experience story known to date.

"While on the 'other side' Mellen journeyed through several realms of consciousness and beyond the 'light at the end of the tunnel.' He was shown during his NDE, in holographic detail, Earth's past and a beautiful vision of mankind's future for the next 400 years. He experienced the cosmology of our soul's connection to mother earth (Gaia), our role in the Universe, and was gifted with access to Universal Intelligence.

"Since his near-death experience, Mellen-Thomas has maintained his direct access to Universal Intelligence, and returns to the light at will, enabling him to be a bridge between science and spirit. He has been involved in research programs on near-death experiences and has developed new technologies for health and wellness. With humil-

> If I chose to continue with the Light I knew that I would die and never return to earth. . . . I thought that I still had important things to do back there [on earth]. At that point the Light began to recede. I found myself waking up on the bed of my dorm room."

ity, insight, and depth of feeling he shares his experience and insights.

"He brings back a message of hope and inspiration for humanity about Life After Death and Reincarnation delivered with a joy and clarity that is refreshing. His depth of feeling and passion for life is a gift to be shared."[4]

> To be *near* completion isn't to be completed. Or to be a *near* genius still isn't to be a genius. And to be "near" death isn't the same as to be dead.

Another person spoke about meeting dead relatives during his near-death experience:

"I noticed that as I began to discern different figures in the light—and they were all covered with light—they were light and had light permeating all around them—they began to form shapes I could recognize and understand. I could see that one of them was my grandmother. I don't know if it was reality or projection, but I would know my grandmother, the sound of her, anytime, anywhere. Everyone I saw, looking back on it, fit perfectly into my understanding of what that person looked like at their best during their lives. I recognized a lot of people. My uncle Gene was there. So was my great-great-aunt Maggie, who was really a cousin. On Papa's side of the family, my grandfather was there. They were specifically taking care of me, looking after me."[5]

How does one reconcile such experiences (often carefully documented) with what the Bible says about death?

NEAR FREE OF MAD COW DISEASE

First of all, consider the very name of the phenomenon: near-death experiences (NDEs). Notice, they're only *near* death, and to be *near* something isn't the same as to be that thing. To be *near* completion isn't to be completed. Or to be a *near* genius still isn't to be a genius. And to be "near" death isn't the same as to be dead.

Sure, the heart and breathing stop. But only for a *very* short while, a few minutes at the most. Therefore, because none underwent rigor mortis or decomposition, we must be careful about what we conclude from NDEs about death, just as we must be careful about what we conclude about alcoholism after taking just one sip of wine. Also, if you wouldn't eat a cut of beef deemed *near* free from mad cow disease, then why build a case for what happens at death based on what's deemed *near* death?

Medical science, meanwhile, has posited various physiological factors that could explain the phenomenon. Though no one knows for sure what's happening, researchers have come up with possibilities that could, from a physical/chemical perspective, solve the question of NDEs. In other words, they could be purely natural experiences,

©PHOTODISC

No one would eat a cut of beef deemed *near* free from mad cow disease.

explained through biochemicals and the suppressed activity of the nervous system alone, without any supernatural element at all.

NEW AGE TEACHINGS

Even if, however, one were to accept the popular notion that at death people immediately go to heaven or hell, why do most come back from NDEs with no sense of a need for Christ or for His gift of salvation? If these people really did go to heaven and talk to God's angels, or to other dead, or even to God Himself, then why didn't the angels, or the dead, or even the Lord tell them about the need for Christ to cover their sins, one of the most basic biblical teachings? Many of those reporting the experience were not professing Christians when they "died," and they rarely come back as ones either. Why? Because in most cases nothing happened during their NDEs that prompted them to accept Christ.

> If one were to accept the popular notion that at death people immediately go to heaven or hell, why do most come back from near-death experiences with no sense of a need for Christ or for His gift of salvation?

Instead (and this should be the clearest warning!) they claim that the spiritual beings they encountered gave them comforting words about love, peace, and goodness, but nothing about salvation in Christ, nothing about sin, and nothing about judgment—again, some of the most fundamental biblical views. One would think that while getting a taste of the Christian afterlife, they should have received at least some of the most basic Christian teachings. Yet so often what they're told sounds more like New Age dogma, which could explain why, in many cases, they come away less inclined toward Christianity than they were before having "died."

COMMON FACTORS IN NEAR-DEATH EXPERIENCES

Listed below are a number of the common elements that fit a general profile for the near-death experience. Some people have reported all of them, while others, only a few.

1. A feeling of peace and quiet overcomes them, a cessation of pain at this point, floating out of their body, seeing the room they are in.

2. Suddenly they are drawn through a dark tunnel, accompanied by a loud noise.

3. They see friends, family, other people, or angel types who welcome them and help them along while comforting them.

4. At the end they reach the light and encounter a being of light that makes them feel loved and unafraid.

5. At this point they have a life review, where every detail of their life is recalled. There is no judgment, only understanding of what and why.

6. They reach a boundary or border over which they cannot pass. They learn many things and see and hear beautiful things, some of which are forgotten when they return.

7. Some are given the option to return, while others are told they must return because it is not their time. Those that refuse to return are ejected, and they return to their bodies reluctantly.

8. Upon return, many experience disappointment; some, depression. Pain, if present before, returns.

9. Transformation takes place in their lives, more spiritual, less materialistic and religious. They're no longer afraid of death. Some talk about it, while others keep it to themselves.[6]

(WWW.NEWAGEDIRECTORY.COM)

If that doesn't sound New Age, then what does? In fact, some of the phenomena associated with NDEs are so similar to the occult and to New Age teachings that a number of Christians—even those who believe that at death people go immediately to heaven or hell—have sounded warnings about NDEs.

The most popular Christian magazine in America, for instance (written by people who hold the common view of death), has warned: "In this and other respects, the NDE phenomenon conforms to recurring New Age aspirations and predilections."[7] The magazine gets right to the heart of the issue (again, even without the safety that comes from understanding the true state of the dead). Because NDEs

SATANIC DECEPTIONS

- "But even if we, or an angel from heaven, preach any other gospel to you than what we have preached to you, let him be accursed" (Galatians 1:8).

- "Be sober, be vigilant; because your adversary the devil walks about like a roaring lion, seeking whom he may devour" (1 Peter 5:8).

- "And war broke out in heaven: Michael and his angels fought against the dragon; and the dragon and his angels fought, but they did not prevail, nor was a place found for them in heaven any longer. So the great dragon was cast out, that serpent of old, called the Devil, and Satan, who deceives the whole world" (Revelation 12:7-9).

Satan deceives the whole world? How? By, among other things, making billions believe that the dead, in one realm or another, are still alive. Satan's first lie to Eve, "You will not surely die" (Genesis 3:4), worked really well then, so why not keep it going? And what better way than using near-death experiences?

rarely make those who experience them feel any need for Christ, the magazine said: "Given what Jesus taught about demonic deception, it makes sense that the Evil One would delight in convincing souls that they need not fear the judgment of a holy God."[8]

ONCE MORE THE CONFLICT BETWEEN GOOD AND EVIL

It makes *great* sense, in fact.

Remember the struggle between good and evil, Christ and Satan, and the fact that Satan is seeking to deceive and to destroy as many as possible. Near-death experiences, and the conclusions that millions have drawn from them, are turning into one of his most effective means of fostering that deception.

Think about it. As long as anyone believes that at death the soul continues to survive in one form or another, then that person is wide open to most occult or spiritualistic deceptions, deceptions that can easily promote the idea, either openly or by implication, that you don't need Jesus. After all, if during an NDE or a séance you see blasphemous and unbelieving Uncle Louie having as much fun in death as he did in his lecherous life, are you going to be more inclined to accept Christ, or less?

（KNOCKING ON HEAVEN'S DOOR?）

The person, however, who understands that the dead are unconscious, knowing nothing, will never fall into one of Satan's most effective and dangerous traps, the concept of the inherent immortality of the soul, the idea that our soul or spirit is an undying consciousness that exists forever. Contrary to popular belief, the Bible does not teach the existence of an immortal soul, either. How could it, in light of all the passages that show, unequivocally, that death is an unconscious sleep?

> The Bible does not teach the existence of an immortal soul. How could it, in light of all the passages that show, unequivocally, that death is an unconscious sleep?

GOD ALONE IS IMMORTAL

Scripture declares: "God, the blessed and only Ruler, the King of kings and Lord of lords, *who alone is immortal* and who lives in unapproachable light" (1 Timothy 6:15, 16, NIV). How could that verse be true if human souls are immortal as well?

Immortality, far from being inherent, comes to us at the Second Coming, at the resurrection of the dead. Discussing the resurrection, Paul states: "For the perishable must clothe itself with the imperishable, and the mortal with immortality. When the perishable has been clothed with the imperishable, and the mortal with immortality, then the saying that is written will come true: 'Death has been swallowed up in victory'" (1 Corinthians 15:53, 54, NIV). If our souls are immortal, enduring forever, what is he talking about? How can death be swallowed up in victory at the Second Coming if those souls, or some sort of conscious spirit, are already alive in heaven?

Elsewhere Paul speaks of God in the judgment giving "eternal life to those who by patient continuance in doing good *seek for glory, honor, and immortality*" (Romans 2:7). Why should we seek immortality if we already have it?

SPIRIT IN THE NOSE

What about such passages as the one in which Stephen, facing death, cries out: "Lord Jesus, receive my spirit" (Acts 7:59)? Doesn't it imply some sort of conscious entity going off to God at death?

Not if "spirit" is simply the mysterious God-given power or force that gives us life. Job's speech includes "all the while my breath is in me, and the spirit of God is in my nostrils" (Job 27:3, KJV). The spirit of God in his nostrils? Funny place for an immortal conscious soul to reside, is it not? Sounds more like a life-giving agent than the entity in which our thoughts, emotions, and consciousness exist. In the Genesis creation account God breathed into Adam's "nostrils" (Genesis 2:7) the breath of life—and it's that life-giving breath that returns to God at death.

"You [God] take away their *breath*, they die and return to their dust" (Psalm 104:29). "Then the dust will return to the earth as it was, and the *spirit* will return to God who gave it" (Ecclesiastes 12:7). "Breath" and "spirit" here are the same thing, and neither is a conscious entity composed of our thoughts, memories, and mental abilities. In both texts the Hebrew term translated "breath" and "spirit" is the same word, one that means "wind" or "breath" or "spirit." It's just a way of expressing the idea that God gave us life, and when we die that life goes back to God.

When announcing the Flood, which would destroy all living things on the earth, God said: "And, behold, I Myself am bringing the flood of waters on the

> "Breath" and "spirit" here are the same thing, and neither is a conscious entity composed of our thoughts, memories, and mental abilities.

Scripture says that even birds have *nephesh*, the Hebrew word used for "soul."

earth, to destroy from under heaven all flesh in which is the *breath of life;* everything that is on the earth shall die" (Genesis 6:17). The word for "breath" is the same used in the two previous texts, and has nothing to do with an immortal conscious entity that continues in another realm after bodily death. Again, it's merely talking about "life" itself.

The Bible never teaches the immortality of the soul. The common word in the Hebrew Bible for "soul" (*nephesh*) means "life, living being, self." In Genesis it's all but synonymous for "man" or "human being." "And man became a living soul *(nephesh hayah)*" (Genesis 2:7, KJV) or "living being" (NIV and other modern translations). "Man" became a "living soul"—that was what he was. Genesis also employs the same phrase for the swarms of "living creatures" *(nephesh hayah)* that God also created (verse 19). So *nephesh* can be "soul," "living being," or "creatures." The book of Genesis uses the same phrase for all the animals, even the birds: "And to all the beasts of the earth and all the birds of the air and all the creatures that move on the ground—everything that has the breath of life *(nephesh hayah)* in it—I give every green plant for food" (Genesis 1:30, NIV). So unless one is going to ascribe immortal souls to cows and cardinals, we have no reason to attribute it to humanity as well.

PAGAN ORIGINS

We can trace the idea of the soul's immortality to various pagan faiths, though it took stronger hold in the Western world through the ancient Greeks, particularly Plato, who wrote: "Of course you know that when a person dies, ... it is natural for the visible and physical part of him . . . to decay and fall to pieces and be dissipated. . . . But the soul, the invisible part, ... goes away to a place that is, like itself, glorious, pure, invisible."[9]

In another dialogue Plato tried to prove, rationally, the immortality of the soul, arguing that the soul existed eternally in the past and continues eternally in the future. For proof he asked a friend's uneducated slave to reason out certain truths about squares and triangles (Plato loved geometry). The slave did so, and on his own, too. How, Plato asked, could an uneducated lad do such a thing unless his soul, in a previous existence, already knew these truths, which were now lodged in his mind via the soul? The slave simply recollected what was already there, even before his birth.

Raphael's Plato in the *School of Athens* fresco, probably in the likeness of Leonardo da Vinci.

"Thus the soul," Plato claimed, "since it is immortal and has been born many times, and has seen all things both here and in the other world, has learned everything that is."[10]

Yet one could just as easily argue, logically, *against* the immortality of soul and the idea of it as some conscious entity existing apart from the body—all based on how inseparable the supposed functions of the "soul" are to the body. If the soul were, in essence, a separate entity from flesh and bone (a "ghost in a machine," as some have called it), why are thoughts, moods, emotions, and self-consciousness, aspects generally associated with the "soul," so drastically affected, even unrecognizably altered, by physical phenomena? Drugs, brain damage, mood elevators, or anything else that alters the physical chemistry or structure of the mind radically changes all the attributes linked to the "soul." This would not make sense were the soul existing in and of itself, somehow independent of the body. Whatever consciousness is, it has a physical component without which it cannot exist, a reality that doesn't bode well for the soul's supposed survival apart from the body.

> Whatever consciousness is, it has a physical component without which it cannot exist, a reality that doesn't bode well for the soul's supposed survival apart from the body.

Whether logical or illogical, belief in the immortality of the soul, of some conscious entity that can exist independent of the body, rages today, manifesting itself in all sorts of religious beliefs, particularly in various New Age and occult teachings.

And, unfortunately, much of Christianity has bought into it as well. This false doctrine has become all but dogma, seen in the common idea that at death the soul flies off immediately to bliss in heaven or torture in hell. It's a view that's not only contradictory to Scripture but denudes one of the most crucial teachings in Scripture—the Second Coming—of its real power and hope. After all, who really cares about the Second Coming if, at death, the saved are already enjoying the presence of the Lord in heaven?

On the other hand, if—as Scripture so clearly teaches—the dead are in an unconscious sleep, then the second coming of Christ takes on a whole new meaning. It acquires the hope that Paul gives it when he wrote: "Listen, I tell you a mystery: We will not all sleep, but we will all be changed—in a flash, in the twinkling of an eye, at the last trumpet. For the trumpet will sound, the dead will be raised imperishable, and we will be changed. For the perishable must clothe itself with the imperishable, and the mortal with immortality. When the perishable has been clothed with the imperishable, and the mortal with immortality, then the saying that is written will come true: 'Death has been swallowed up in victory.' 'Where, O death, is your victory? Where, O death, is your sting?'" (1 Corinthians 15:51-55, NIV).

THE BOTTOM LINE

In an earlier chapter we asked ourselves, What's the point of redemption, of salvation, and of eternal life if we're all just dead men and women walking? As we've seen, we're all sinners, having violated God's law and all been condemned by that law. But that's precisely why Jesus came: To save us from the condemnation that our breaking of the law brings. And He did it by keeping the law perfectly and then offering to us His perfect record, which becomes ours by faith when we claim it for ourselves. As a result our condemnation stands revoked, and we have all those promises of eternal life.

> Unless someone or something solves the problem of death, we're all doomed to eternal oblivion, fated to meaningless and purposelessness.

We understand the promises of salvation, redemption, and eternal life, because we have the assurance of the Second Coming, with its resurrection of the dead, when Christ brings to fruition the promises He made at His first advent. Unless someone or something solves the problem of death, we're all doomed to eternal oblivion, fated to meaninglessness and purposelessness—a tough conclusion for beings who are capable of conceiving of eternity, of infinity, of something greater our own short lives, because we can contrast those lives to the concept of eternity.

Yet the great news is that eternity won't leave us behind, won't unfurl forever without us. Instead, thanks to Jesus, we'll be part of eternity, an eternity in which we'll have new bodies in a new existence, one in which the conflict between good and evil has finally ceased, Satan is no more, and we will be as God had originally intended for us to be—healthy, happy creatures growing in the knowledge of His goodness and love.

This is the great Christian hope, not a hope in ourselves or in nature, but one that transcends anything and everything this world has to offer.

A hope founded on Jesus, and on Him alone.

---

[1] http://www.washingtonmonthly.com/features/2003/0306.green.html.

[2] http://www.answers.com/topic/royal-intermarriage.

[3] http://paranormal.about.com/library/weekly/aa082800a.htm.

[4] http://www.mellen-thomas.com.

[5] http://paranormal.about.com/library/weekly/aa082800b.htm.

[6] http://www.newagedirectory.com/nde/nde_profile.htm.

[7] *Christianity Today,* Apr. 3, 1995, p. 41.

[8] *Ibid.,* p. 42.

[9] Plato, *Collected Dialogues.,* ed. Edith Hamilton and Huntington Cairns (Princeton, N.J.: Princeton University Press, 1961), pp. 63, 64.

[10] *Ibid.,* p. 364.

ARE YOU JESUS?

A PLANE TO CATCH

*A*fter a convention in a foreign city, a pack of high-powered six-figured-salary executives rushed through an airport to catch a jet home. Suddenly one of them accidentally caught the edge of a table filled with apples that tumbled awkwardly across the floor. The one who hit the table glanced at the carnage unfolding behind his heels, but, ever fighting the clock, he never lost his momentum. The others didn't turn around at all.

Except one. Pausing, he glanced at the

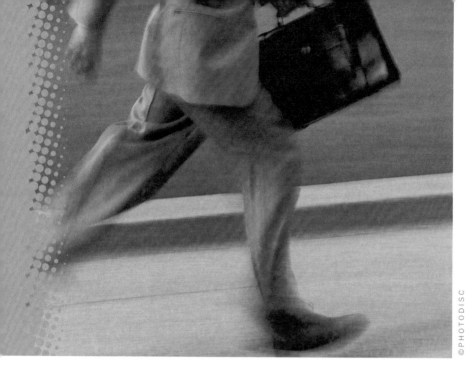

Life is more than just a plane to catch.

turmoil they had left, and then back at the shrinking figures of his fellow executives. When they noticed that he was no longer with them, they stopped and turned around, looking as if they were thinking, *What are you doing? We have a plane to catch!* Reading their expressions, he answered, "Go on ahead. I will see you back in the States on Monday."

Hesitating, they stared at him and then, with a collective shrug, vanished. With them gone, he glanced at the girl whose apple stand had collapsed. She wore glasses with lenses as thick as soda bottle bottoms, and her eyes—distorted in size by the dirty and scratched glass—filled with tears as she groped for her fallen wares. An apple practically had to be touching her face before she could see it.

The executive told her to calm down, that he would get all the apples. She looked toward him, her eyes filled with wonderment and pain. He wasn't sure how much of him she could see. Setting the rickety stand back up, he gathered the apples and put them back. The ones too bruised to sell he dumped into a garbage can. Finished, he pulled out his wallet and handed her $100, saying that this was for the damage and trouble they had caused. She clutched the money in her hand, holding the bills and appearing as if she couldn't quite believe what she couldn't quite see.

"OK," he said, "I have to go. I hope everything is fine now."

Lowering the money from in front of her eyes, she peered at him. Again, he wasn't quite sure what she saw.

"Is everything OK now?" he asked.

She squeezed the money tighter.

"I have to go."

She nodded and, as he left, called out, "Please, sir."

He turned around and answered, "Yes?"

"Sir, are you Jesus?"

RESTORATION

No, he wasn't Jesus—not even close. But her naive question revealed an important truth about Jesus. All through this book we have looked at such things as the meaning of life, the cross, the cosmic struggle between Christ and Satan, the plan of salvation, the hope of the Second Coming, and the promise of eternity in a new world, because no matter how hard we try or how good our intentions, this world guarantees us only one thing—death.

Yet being a follower of Jesus isn't just about the hope of something beyond this life. Christianity would mean nothing, of course, were there no hope after our present existence. But being a follower of Jesus also means nothing if it doesn't change our lives here. "I have come," Jesus said, "that they may have life, and that they may have it more abundantly" (John 10:10), and that's not just eternal life but our present existence. Jesus wants us to live more abundantly *now*. He longs to gives us a foretaste of what we will someday have, only infinitely better and for eternity.

Unlike some religions, the Bible does not teach that the human body is itself evil. Nor does it claim, as some ancient philosophies have, that our existence in our bodies is a punishment, that as higher disembodied spirits we were cast down to earth in the prison of flesh as a penalty for some ethereal transgression. On the contrary, the opening chapter of Genesis shows that our world and the beings in it—especially human beings—were created good, the deliberate and purposeful act of God.

Our Fall wasn't *to* flesh—rather, it was, instead, a Fall *in* the flesh, one that started *from* the flesh and that leads to us losing that flesh, which is what death is all about. Death, the enemy, is a dissolution of what God created for us, which is our physical bodies. That dissolution was never God's plan. He created us to live forever, and in the flesh, too. God's plan is to restore our flesh, giving us a body that never sees corruption, pain, or suffering again.

The plan of salvation is *restoration*. God wants to bring us back to what we were originally to be, at least as much as possible now. And the good news is that we don't have to wait until the Second Coming for that restoration to start. It begins when we accept Jesus. A new life commences for us then. It is a change, a process, that commences here and now and that's completed when Christ returns.

PROMISES OF RESTORATION

- "His intent was that now, through the church, the manifold wisdom of God should be made known to the rulers and authorities in the heavenly realms" (Ephesians 3:10, NIV).

- "Do you not know that as many of us as were baptized into Christ Jesus were baptized into His death? Therefore we were buried with Him through baptism into death, that just as Christ was raised from the dead by the glory of the Father, even so we also should walk in newness of life" (Romans 6:3, 4).

- "Therefore, if anyone is in Christ, he is a new creation; old things have passed away; behold, all things have become new" (2 Corinthians 5:17).

- "Being confident of this very thing, that He who has begun a good work in you will complete it until the day of Jesus Christ" (Philippians 1:6).

- "I will give you a new heart and put a new spirit within you; I will take the heart of stone out of your flesh and give you a heart of flesh" (Ezekiel 36:26).

- "My little children, for whom I labor in birth again until Christ is formed in you" (Galatians 4:19).

Without question, the process of change starts now, in this life. It isn't a physical restoration, though that can be part of it, because God is a healing Lord, even if full and complete physical transformation will occur only at the second coming of Jesus and the resurrection. Then, and only then, will the physical damage caused by sin to our flesh be fully erased.

The present restoration, instead, is moral. Spiritual in nature and transforming the character, it greatly improves the quality of our lives here while preparing us for life in a new heaven and a new earth. Although we have been born, raised, and nurtured in a world reeking in violence, hatred, lust, greed, and sin, we can still start the naturalization process for a world in which none of these things exist.

THE STORY OF IVAN THE FOOL

Leo Tolstoy penned a tale called "The Story of Ivan the Fool." It told of three bothers, one of whom was greedy for money, one for power, and one, "a fool," greedy for nothing and who always let others take advantage of him. In Tolstoy's story the devil and his imps seek to destroy the family, to bring disharmony and discord among them. "Now you three go," the devil directed some imps, "and tackle those three brothers, and worry them till they scratch each other's eyes out."[1]

They have great success with the first two brothers, using their greed and weaknesses to ruin them, but nothing the imps do can ruin Ivan the fool, who—though taken advantage of again and again—

never falls into their traps because he's too simple, too naive, too innocent to take the bait. In the end Ivan not only thrives but takes care of his brothers, who have been ruined by their own character defects. "Ivan is still living," the story ends, "and people crowd to his kingdom. His own brothers have come to live with him, and he feeds them, too."[2]

Leo Tolstoy

PUBLIC DOMAIN

Though only a fantasy, Tolstoy's story reveals an important spiritual truth, one expressed, perhaps, best by the apostle Paul when he wrote: "We are fools for Christ's sake" (1 Corinthians 4:10). By the world's standards the Christian ideals of meekness, of humility, of turning the other cheek, of forgiveness, of even love to one's enemies, make followers of Jesus appear as fools.

And yet, look at what *the world judges them by!* It's a standard in which greed, lust, hatred, violence, jealousy, and the desire for gain and for power and prestige rules. *This is the criteria that mock the Christian characteristics of purity, humility, love, and forgiveness?* It's as if a prostitute, dying of AIDS, taunts a healthy young virgin for being a prude.

THOUGHT EXPERIMENT

Scientists often perform thought experiments, in which they envision situations that aren't practical to duplicate. Let's try one. Let's envision this world, only instead of greed, pride, prejudice, avarice, revenge, sexual immorality, violence, and terror being the norm, the Christian virtues of forgiveness, compassion, humility, love, and self-denial are. How different would that world be from the one we live in now? Which would you prefer to live in: the one of the experiment, or the one of reality? Would you prefer to raise children in the world in which Christian values rule, or the one ruled by greed, lust, violence, and pride?

The answer's obvious. God has given us a moral code—a standard of how to live—to make our lives, not miserable, but better. Thousands of years ago He told ancient Israel "to keep the commandments of the Lord and His statutes which I command you today *for your good*" (Deuteronomy 10:13). For whose good? For theirs, and for all those who honored that law.

It's the same today. God wants to give us a better life here. He longs to spare us so much of the suffering that our sins bring upon ourselves and others. But He can do it only if we obey His law, especially its core, the Ten Commandments. God's law can't do us any

©PHOTODISC

"I know that God forgives my sin, but the consequences don't go away as easily."

good if we ignore it, any more than a regulation against drunk driving can protect people against drunk driving unless they follow it.

A Christian at his 30-year high school reunion met people that he hadn't seen since the 1970s. As he looked at the wreckage of their lives, their pain, sickness, and suffering (so much of it brought upon themselves or by others around them) one thought entered his mind as he left: "Thank God for the Ten Commandments." He was intensely aware of the great protection found in following the divine commandments.

A social worker in south Philadelphia told of a girl, 14 years old and heavy with child, who walked into a health clinic. Tears streaming down her eyes, she said, "I know that God forgives my sin, but"—she stared down at her swollen belly—"the consequences don't go away as easily."

No, they don't, do they? It would be bad enough if the consequences of our sins, of our disobedience, hurt only ourselves. But it doesn't operate that way. As we saw earlier in this book, we aren't islands—we don't live in isolation. Our words, our deeds, and our attitudes emanate from us more powerfully and further than does our breath and body odor. And the ones our deeds hurt the most are usually those closest to us. They feel the full brunt of our transgressions.

An alcoholic father leaves his young daughter in a parked car while he goes into a bar and drinks for hours, forgetting about the child; after hours in the freezing car, she loses hearing in both ears. A woman, committing adultery, develops a case of genital herpes that in childbirth gets transmitted to her newborn, damaging the infant's brain for life. A teenager, stealing money for drugs, goes to prison, bringing his grieving parents almost to the edge of the grave. A father, sexually abused as a child, sexually abuses his own offspring . . .

The list goes on, and on, and on.

THE MORPHINE FACTOR

That's why God has given us His moral law, His Ten Commandments. If kept, they form a wall of protection, a hedge that shelters us from so much of the pain and suffering that their violation brings. God's law isn't to oppress us—it's to free us from the horrible consequences that sin inevitably causes.

Ask the mother whose adultery led to her newborn's brain damage how oppressive she now thinks the Ten Commandments

> God's moral law, His Ten Commandments, forms a wall of protection, a hedge that shelters us from so much of the pain and suffering that their violation brings.

are. (We'd like to ask her grown child, too, but the retardation is so severe that he wouldn't know what we were talking about.) Maybe we could question the 12-year-old boy whose life came apart after his dad destroyed the family by running off with the neighbor's daughter whether he considers the Ten Commandments restrictive. Or perhaps we could interview some of the thousands of people murdered around the world each year about their opinion of the Ten Commandments (but of course we can't, because they're all dead).

The Ten Commandments restrictive? oppressive? Yes. But so are laws against pedophilia, rape, car theft, murder, and incest. The Ten Commandments are restrictive in the same way that a parent who forbids his or her children from playing in traffic is restrictive.

How limiting to our freedom—those signs that warn us from wandering across a minefield! How oppressive against the individual rights of airline pilots that they aren't allowed to fly commercial jets drunk! How unfair to our freedom those laws that regulate speed limits! And—how restricting that God has a moral law that He commands us to obey!

> Jesus' death on the cross proved the perpetuity and immutability of the law, because if the law could have been changed to meet us in our fallen condition, then He wouldn't have had to die for us.

As shown earlier, only the righteousness of Jesus Christ—which He wrought out in His perfect life, and which He offers to us as a gift—can bring us salvation. But the fact that we are not saved by keeping God's law doesn't mean that we're still not commanded by God to obey it. Jesus' death on the cross proved the perpetuity and immutability of the law, because if the law could have been changed to meet us in our fallen condition, then He wouldn't have had to die for us. He could have just altered it rather than sacrificing Himself because of our violation of it. The cross is the greatest proof of the validity of the Ten Commandments, which is why the New Testament makes it clear that we are to still keep them:

OBEDIENCE TO GOD'S COMMANDMENTS

- "His intent was that now, through the church, the manifold wisdom of God should be made known to the rulers and authorities in the heavenly realms" (Ephesians 3:10, NIV).

- "Do you not know that as many of us as were baptized into Christ Jesus were baptized into His death? Therefore we were buried with Him through baptism into death, that just as Christ was raised from the dead by the glory of the Father, even so we also should walk in newness of life" (Romans 6:3, 4).

- "For this is the love of God, that we keep His commandments. And His commandments are not burdensome" (1 John 5:3).

- "Now by this we know that we know Him, if we keep His commandments. He who says, 'I know Him,' and does not keep His commandments, is a liar, and the truth is not in him" (1 John 2:3, 4).

- "For whoever shall keep the whole law, and yet stumble in one point, he is guilty of all. For He who said, 'Do not commit adultery,' also said, 'Do not murder.' Now if you do not commit adultery, but you do murder, you have become a transgressor of the law" (James 2:10, 11).

- "Circumcision is nothing and uncircumcision is nothing, but keeping the commandments of God is what matters" (1 Corinthians 7:19).

- "Here is the patience of the saints; here are those who keep the commandments of God and the faith of Jesus" (Revelation 14:12).

Morphine can't save a dying patient's life, but it sure can make that person's existence better in the meantime. Keeping the law won't save us from sin, but it can make our life in our sinful world a far less painful experience. That's why God calls us to obey His law—it's for our own good. Obedience doesn't guarantee that pain and suffering won't come to us or to our loved ones—it only ensures that we are less likely to cause that suffering ourselves.

THE GOD WITH PALE LIPS

A train explosion in North Korea had left more than 160 people dead. The North Korean news agency that reported the blast told about the heroic efforts of some citizens who risked, and in some cases even lost, their lives in attempts to save from the burning buildings portraits of North Korean leader Kim Jong-il and his deceased father, Kim Il-sung.

> We worship what we live for, what we believe is important, what we think gives meaning to our lives. And we worship what we consider "divine," even if what we deem divine isn't necessarily deity.

"Upon hearing of the sound of the heavy explosion on their way home for lunch, Choe Yong-il and Jon Tong-sik, workers at the County Procurement Shop, ran back to the shop. They were buried under the collapsing building and died a heroic death when they were trying to come out with portraits of President Kim Il-sung and leader Kim Jong-il. . . .

"Teacher Han Jong-suk, fifty-six, also breathed her last with portraits in her bosom. . . .

"Such a noble deed was also done by head of the county nursery Pak Sun-mi and seven nurses. . . . Many people of the county evacuated portraits before searching for their family members or saving their household goods."[3]

There's something innate in human beings, something perhaps originally wired in us but damaged in the Fall, that make us want to worship something—*anything*. And "anything" means just that, *any*thing—from bulls and frogs to pop stars; from Roman emperors to Korean dictators; from the sun and moon to money, fame, power, and even ourselves. We worship what we live for, what we believe is important, what we think gives meaning to our lives. And we worship what we consider "divine," even if what we deem divine isn't necessarily deity. On the contrary, so often humans worship the gods of their own making, gods unable to answer the deepest needs of this life, much less offer us anything for the next.

In Shakespeare's *Julius Caesar,* Brutus and Cassius discuss the plot to kill Caesar. Here's a paraphrase of what Cassius said:

"I was born as free as Caesar; so were you;
We eat the same foods, and we can both
Stand the winter's cold just as well as Caesar.
One time, on a cold and windy day,
When the Tiber River was rising in the storm,
Caesar said to me, 'Cassius, I dare you
To leap with me into this angry flood
And swim to that spot way over there.' As soon as he said it,
Dressed like I was, I plunged in
And dared him to follow. That's exactly what he did.
The torrent roared, and we fought it
With strong muscles, throwing it aside
And conquering it with our spirit of competition.
But before we could arrive at the designated spot,
Caesar cried, 'Help me, Cassius, or I will sink!'
Just like Aeneas, our great ancestor,
Carried the old Anchises from the flames of Troy
On his shoulder, I from the waves of Tiber
Carried the tired Caesar. And this man
Is now considered a god, and Cassius is
A wretched creature and must bow down
If Caesar even carelessly nods at him.
He had a fever when he was in Spain,
And when he was having fits, I saw clearly
How he shook. It is true, this god shook.
His lips turned pale,
And that same eye whose glance awes the world
Lost his shine. I heard him groan.
Yes, and that tongue of his that persuaded the Romans
To watch him closely and write his speeches in their books,
Alas, it cried, 'Give me something to drink, Titinius,'
Just like a sick girl! You gods! It amazes me
That such a weak man should

Gaius Cassius Longinus featured on a denarius (42 B.C.).

GNU FDL

Get ahead of the rest of the world
And appear as the victor all by himself."[4]

At least Cassius learned what so many others might not find out until it's too late, and that's just how weak, impotent, and human all our false gods are.

No Other Gods

Perhaps that's why the first commandment reads simply, "You shall have no other gods before Me" (Exodus 20:3). There are, in fact, no other gods at all, except the ones of our own devising. The Lord, who created us, alone deserves worship. From single-celled plants to the sinews that hold our bones together, it all comes from Him, and because He wants us to know this truth He gave us this commandment right from the start, the foundation of all that follows.

Writer and philosopher Bertrand Russell spent time in jail for his opposition to World War I. His jailer, making small talk, asked Russell what religion he was. "I'm an agnostic," Bertrand replied. Not exactly the most educated of individuals, the jailer looked at him askance at first and then brightened up, replying, "I guess it's all right. We all worship the same God, don't we?"

No, we don't. There's only one God, the deity who created the world, and because He's the Creator He's entitled to be first in our lives. That's why, when asked about the greatest commandment, Jesus said: "Thou shalt love the Lord thy God with all thy heart, and with all thy soul, and with all thy mind. This is the first and great commandment" (Matthew 22:37, KJV). And how can you do that if there's any other "god" before Him?

Notice, too, that Jesus said this was "the first . . . commandment." But doesn't the first commandment read: "You shall have no other gods before Me"? That's precisely the point. Jesus is basically interpreting the first commandment, saying that it means you will love the Lord your God with everything you have because everything you have comes from Him.

No Graven Images

Directly tied in with the first commandment is the second: "You shall not make for yourself a carved image—any likeness of anything that is in heaven above, or that is in the earth beneath, or that is in the water under the earth; you shall not bow down to them nor serve them. For I, the Lord your God, am a jealous God, visiting the iniquity of the fathers upon the children to the third and fourth generations of those who hate Me, but showing mercy to thousands, to those who love Me and keep My commandments" (Exodus 20:4-6).

The Lord gave this command to Israel at a time that their neighbors were steeped in idolatry, and though most people today don't bow before statues of frogs and bulls, the world's just as idolatrous now as when the Israelites wandered in the Sinai desert. What's worse is that the idols and the false gods worshipped today are just as empty, vain, and dangerous as when the ancients worshipped statues of the Egyptian cat goddess.

Why should God care about people worshipping idols? Creator of the universe and sustainer of the entire cosmos, couldn't He handle beings on our tiny planet worshipping something other than Himself?

The answer's simple: God loves us (as He proved by sending Jesus), and He knows that people can't rise higher than what they worship and serve. The pagan nations around ancient Israel participated in the most degrading religious practices, everything from temple prostitution to the sacrificing of their children on altars. If they worshipped gods who were like the animals, then how much higher than animals would they themselves rise?

In the same way, those who worship Michael Jackson, Britney Spears, or whoever the latest pop star is aren't going to become much higher morally than any of

PUBLIC DOMAIN

The Reagans and Michael Jackson at a White House ceremony, 1984.

them. But whether Michael Jackson or Jackson Browne, whether money, or fame, or success, when they become idols, the objects of worship, who needs a prophet to see that only carnage will be left in their wake? But because God loves us, He wants so much more for us. He longs for us to aspire to the highest levels possible, and thus spare ourselves the kind of suffering that living as moral bottom-feeders inevitably brings. Such moral elevation can result only as we worship, serve, and obey Him, not the idols of our own making.

THE DACHAU FACTOR

Someone visiting the Nazi concentration camp of Dachau told how a guide began the tour by discussing Charles Darwin and the theory of evolution. According to the guide, the Nazis' racial policies derived from the idea of the "survival of the fittest," the teaching that

Gates at the main entrance to Dachau concentration camp, 1945, just after the liberation.

all species are in a constant life-and-death battle for survival, and only the strongest or best adapted endure. Over time these ideas became the foundation of Social Darwinism, which viewed some humans as stronger, more racially advanced on the evolutionary chain than others, and therefore the inferior versions, which could stand in the way of the advanced ones, needed eliminating. For many, the natural conclusion of such thinking was the Holocaust.

Whether one agrees with the logic, there's no question that the typical evolutionary scenario, in which all life is a product of pure chance, can't help molding people's moral views. Morality would have to be something of our own devising, because there is no one or nothing above us to show us what is truly right or wrong. In contrast, people who believe that we are all beings made in the image of God, a deity who died for the sins of all people, should have a different concept of morality than those who believe that we're the products of pure chance alone, with no inherent purpose or end goal for our lives.

Hence, the importance of the those first two commandments, because as long as we remember that the Lord is God, the Creator, and that He is a moral and a just deity, we are likely to be more circumspect in our actions, knowing that a God of justice exists who will hold us accountable. If, in the Darwinian scheme, no moral authority exists above our own selves, and the ultimate good is our own survival, then the highest morality is to ensure that survival. Thus, if getting rid of inferior races would help advance this highest moral good—then why not?

A TRUE GOD WILL CARE FOR THE WEAK

In contrast, the worship of the true God should lead us to care for the weak, not to dispose of them as hindrances to evolutionary progress. The worship of the true God should move us to treat all human beings—family, friends, the poor, the homeless, our enemies, even—as beings created in the divine image and not as the chance results of time and space. That's why Jesus said, "But I say to you who hear: Love your enemies, do good to those who hate you, bless those

> Jesus didn't preach a survival-of-the-fittest morality. He believed that our worship of the true God should lead to a morality that the worship of frogs or money never could.

who curse you, and pray for those who spitefully use you. To him who strikes you on the one cheek, offer the other also. And from him who takes away your cloak, do not withhold your tunic either. Give to everyone who asks of you. . . . And just as you want men to do to you, you also do to them likewise" (Luke 6:27-31). Or that we should "love your neighbor as yourself" (Mark 12:31), or that we should feed and clothe the needy and hungry because "whatever you did for one of the least of these brothers of mine, you did for me" (Matthew 25:40, NIV).

Clearly (1) Jesus didn't preach a survival-of-the-fittest morality, and (2) He believed that our worship of the true God should lead us to a level of goodness, kindness, and morality that the worship of frogs or money never could.

THE SAVING GOD

But idolatry, the worship of false gods, has still another problem, and we can see it dramatized through a short story, again by Leo Tolstoy, called "How Much Land Does a Man Need?" In it a struggling farmer named Pahom tells himself, "If I had plenty of land, I shouldn't fear the Devil himself."[5] The devil, listening in, silently replies: "We will have a tussle. I will give you land enough; and by means of that land I will get you into my power."[6]

Pahom then hears about the Bashkirs, people who sell land cheaply. Pahom goes to them, and they offer him land for "one thousand rubles a day."[7] As far as he can walk in one day is what he can buy for his 1,000 rubles, but on one condition: "If you don't return," they said, "on the same day to the spot whence you started, your money is lost."[8]

Thrilled, Pahom takes off, marking off the edges of this rich, virgin soil. He keeps going, as far as he possibly can before making a turn. Though covering a lot of land, he soon realizes that he had better get back to his starting point or he'll have none. Exhausted (he had walked so far), he sees that he has no time to lose, that the sun is almost setting. Racing in a panic, Pahom almost reaches where he began, only to collapse—dead.

"The Baskirs clicked their tongues to show their pity."[9]

"His servant picked up the spade and dug a grave long enough for Pahom to lie in, and buried him in it," Tolstoy ended his tale. "Six feet from his head to his heels was all he needed."[10]

Suppose, though, that Pahom—less greedy, less covetous, not having money as his god—instead of dying, reached his starting point before the sun set and so all that land, and all the riches that could have resulted from it, were his? In the end, ultimately, he'd still need only six feet. Death was still waiting, no matter what he accomplished. And in the face of death, how small all one's accomplishments really seem anyway. How insignificant, in fact, they are.

Each of us, like Pahom, is just another twisted, corrupt, selfish sinner crammed with billions of others on a polluted planet whose surface is mostly un-inhabitable salt water. No matter who we are or how wealthy, happy, and content we might be, nature still aims to kill us, and everyone we love, either quickly or slowly, and always without remorse—and it always succeeds, one way or another. No matter how well we organize and plan our lives, careers, finances, families, something lurks out there that can snatch it all away, or damage, twist, and even turn it against us and ruin us both inside out. If, as Benjamin Franklin said, death and taxes are the only sure things in this life, then that leaves a lot of other

PUBLIC DOMAIN

Benjamin Franklin

things—things we love, cherish, and need—no more certain than our chances of winning a super lottery ticket.

THE GOD WHO CAN OVERCOME ENTROPY

We live in a world that in and of itself leads to tragedy for everyone. All its great political causes (that once held out some promise) have failed. It is a world in which everything is moving toward collapse and entropy. By its very nature such a world needs to be saved, and yet humanity—with all its technology and science—can only prolong the agony. It can never end it. All our idols and gods, no matter whatever we think that they can do for us here, can't save us from death. Only the true God, the deity who first gave us life, can.

> All our idols and gods, no matter whatever we think that they can do for us here, can't save us from death. Only the true God, the deity who first gave us life, can.

"'I am the first and I am the last; apart from me there is no God. . . .' All who make idols are nothing, and the things they treasure are worthless. . . . The carpenter measures with a line and makes an outline with a marker; he roughs it out with chisels and marks it with compasses. He shapes it in the form of man, of man in all his glory, that it may dwell in a shrine. He cut down cedars, or perhaps took a cypress or oak. He let it grow among the trees of the forest, or planted a pine, and the rain made it grow. It is man's fuel for burning; some of it he takes and warms himself, he kindles a fire and bakes bread. But he also fashions a god and worships it; he makes an idol and bows down to it. Half of the wood he burns in the fire; over it he prepares his meal, he roasts his meat and eats his fill. He also warms himself and says, 'Ah! I am warm; I see the fire.' From the rest he makes a god, his idol; he bows down to it and worships. He prays to it and says, 'Save me; you are my god'" (Isaiah 44:6-17, NIV).

Save me, because you are my god? Fame, success, money, sex, power—what good will such idols be when family members are picking out our coffins or stuffing our ashes in an urn? The Lord so longed for us to have eternal life that He suffered on the cross. He gave Himself, the best that heaven had to offer, in order to redeem us. And so He doesn't want us throwing it all away on empty, vain, useless things that can't give us the one thing that every human needs—the assurance that death doesn't have to be forever.

IN VAIN

The Talmud, an ancient Jewish commentary on the Bible, tells about a man who sneaks into his neighbor's barn at night and steals wheat. He takes it home, grinds it into flour, bakes it into bread, and then, sitting down to eat, lifts his voice in prayer and says a blessing over the bread. Such a man, the Talmud says, doesn't bless but blasphemes.

Christian speaker Tony Campolo told of being mugged at gunpoint. After the robber took his wallet, he asked his victim, "What kind of work do you do?"

"I'm a Baptist minister," Campolo answered.

"Oh," the thief replied, "you're a Baptist? So am I."

A rabbi tells about a bank robber in Israel who, though right-handed, held his pistol in his left hand during a robbery. Why? So he could, as he walked out with the loot, perform the pious act of touching the mezuzah (a small object kept on doorposts to remind Jews of the law) as he fled.

In each case, what commandment did the individuals violate? It was the third, which reads: "You shall not take the name of the Lord your God in vain, for the Lord will not hold him guiltless who takes His name in vain" (Exodus 20:7). Though, no doubt, the commandment warns against

Mezuzah

using God or His name in a curse, it's so much broader.

We find the key to understanding the commandment in the Hebrew word for "vain," which means, basically, "nothingness," "vanity," "emptiness," "worthlessness." What it's saying, then, is don't take God's name worthlessly. Don't use or profess His name unless you mean it. We could perhaps express the command as: "Don't be a religious hypocrite."

While hypocrisy is bad enough, religious hypocrisy is even worse, which is no doubt why Jesus had the harshest words, not for adulter-

SPIRITUAL HYPOCRISY

"Woe to you, scribes and Pharisees, hypocrites! For you shut up the kingdom of heaven against men; for you neither go in yourselves, nor do you allow those who are entering to go in. Woe to you, scribes and Pharisees, hypocrites! For you devour widows' houses, and for a pretense make long prayers. Therefore you will receive greater condemnation.

"Woe to you, scribes and Pharisees, hypocrites! For you travel land and sea to win one proselyte, and when he is won, you make him twice as much a son of hell as yourselves. . . .

"Woe to you, scribes and Pharisees, hypocrites! For you pay tithe of mint and anise and cummin, and have neglected the weightier matters of the law: justice and mercy and faith. These you ought to have done, without leaving the others undone. Blind guides, who strain out a gnat, and swallow a camel!

"Woe to you, scribes and Pharisees, hypocrites! For you cleanse the outside of the cup and dish, but inside they are full of extortion and self-indulgence. Blind Pharisee, first cleanse the inside of the cup and dish, that the outside of them may be clean also.

"Woe to you, scribes and Pharisees, hypocrites! For you are like whitewashed tombs which indeed appear beautiful outwardly, but inside are full of dead men's bones and all uncleanness. Even so you also outwardly appear righteous to men, but inside you are full of hypocrisy and lawlessness.

"Woe to you, scribes and Pharisees, hypocrites! Because you build the tombs of the prophets and adorn the monuments of the righteous, and say, 'If we had lived in the days of our fathers, we would not have been partakers with them in the blood of the prophets.'

"Therefore you are witnesses against yourselves that you are sons of those who murdered the prophets. Fill up, then, the measure of your fathers' guilt. Serpents, brood of vipers! How can you escape the condemnation of hell?" (Matthew 23:13-33).

ers (John 8:1-11), fornicators (John 4:2-42), thieves (Luke 23:39-43), or even killers (Acts 9:4-6), but for those who cloaked their evil in robes of professed religion and piety.

THE AMISH FACTOR

Jesus didn't speak that strongly to anyone else, not even to prostitutes and thieves. Instead, He condemned those who took His name in vain by seizing the homes of widows while cloaking their thievery under a veneer of long prayers or who performed religious rituals in order to make themselves look pious even though they neglected kindness, mercy, and compassion. He castigated them for their obsession with outward ritual cleanliness that accompanied the Jewish dietary laws while their minds and hearts were full of greed and self-indulgence. All of them were, at the core, breaking the third commandment.

Think what it would be like if all those who claimed to be followers of Christ lived out the principles that He taught. Imagine how much better our homes, our marriages, and our relationships with our children, coworkers, and friends would be if those who took the name of the Lord didn't do it in vain.

During the summer of 2006, in the American state of Pennsylvania, a gunman walked into an Amish schoolhouse, drove out everyone except the girls, and proceeded to murder each one. The thought of those children in their long dresses and bonnets murdered in cold blood wrung the hearts of everyone everywhere.

> **Think what it would be like if all those who claimed to be followers of Christ lived out the principles that He taught.**

Yet everyone, everywhere, also received a powerful lesson in what it means to keep the third commandment. The same Amish, grieving for their dead children,

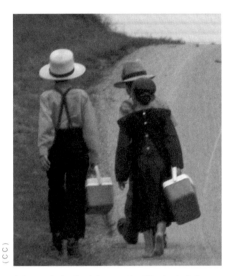

(CC)

A tragedy in Amish country illustrated the power of Christian forgiveness.

called upon their people to forgive the gunman. The grandfather of one dead girl stood before her casket and said, "We are teaching our young people not to think evil of this man." Some Amish even attended the funeral of the killer, and others reached out to the wife and family of the gunman, offering help and support.

What a different world we would live in if all those who claimed the name of the Lord lived it out like that. And the good news is we don't have to wait for everyone else, even other professed Christians, to start doing it. We can ask Christ into our hearts, open ourselves to Him, and then let Him work out His holiness in us starting now. Maybe you can't change the world, but you can make the choice to be changed yourself, a transformation that God will accomplish in our lives if we let Him, one destined to make our lives better even here and now. That's why God has given us His law—to make our lives and existence better—and few things could do that more than adhering to the third commandment.

MACH 9.6

The new world record for jet-powered aircraft is NASA's X-43A scramjet, which came screaming across the sky at Mach 9.6, or nearly 7,000 mph. Though a crawl compared to the X-43A, the fastest land speed record in a car was set in 1997, when the jet-powered Thrust SCC smoked a Nevada desert at 760 miles per hour. And if Columbus had had a rig like the one that set the world's record for a boat (317 miles per hour), America might have already celebrated its tricentennial.

Without question, we're going faster and faster all the time. With the mere flick of a cell phone or click of a mouse we can do what once took weeks, months, even longer. Twenty-five years ago scientists were amazed that a massive mainframe computer could process a billion pieces of information a second (a gigahertz)—the

The X-43A being dropped from under the wing of a B-52B Stratofortress.

speed of the average laptop today. In a few years a billion and a billion and a half computations a second won't be quick enough to run most programs. Some computers are now computing in teraflops (a trillion calculations per second). Eventually CPU speeds measured in gigahertz will be as antiquated as dot-matrix printers.

And though moving at speeds our ancestors would have deemed miraculous, even supernatural, most people complain about the same thing, and that is—not enough time. We're harried and burned out, because no matter what we do and how fast we do it, and no matter where we go or how fast we get there, there's still more to do and more places to go and not enough minutes to accomplish it all. If days were 36 hours it wouldn't matter—we'd still need more. Time is a tyrant that demands all that we have, and we never have enough.

> God carved out an inviolable and indestructible refuge from time's insatiable silent rush that traps us all in its unrelenting flow.

How fascinating, then, that thousands of years ago the Lord gave humanity a commandment designed to protect us from time's tyranny. God carved out an inviolable and indestructible refuge from time's insatiable silent rush that traps us all in its unrelenting flow. Called the Sabbath, it has its origin in the foundation of the world itself—that is, it was part of the original Creation, something as primeval and basic as time itself, because it is part of time.

THE SABBATH COMMANDMENT

In the Genesis creation account God fashioned the earth and sky, and all that's in it, in six days. But what happened next?

"Thus the heavens and the earth, and all the host of them, were finished. And on the seventh day God ended His work which He had done, and He rested on the seventh day from all His work which he had done. Then God blessed the seventh day and sanctified it, because in it He had rested from all His work which God had created and made" (Genesis 2:1-3).

> The commandment ties itself directly to the original six-day creation depicted in Genesis.

Notice several points:

1. God blessed and sanctified the seventh day before the entrance of sin, before the fall of Adam and Eve. The seventh day, as sacred and holy time, came from a perfect world. Therefore, attempts to link it exclusively with the types and symbols and festivals that pointed to Jesus all fail because those things arose *after* the entrance of sin, while the seventh day was sanctified *before* sin.

2. Even more obvious, the seventh day as a holy day predated the Jewish nation by thousands of years. The idea of the seventh-day Sabbath being exclusively Jewish is false. That the Jews took hold of the Sabbath day and have adhered to it is, of course, undeniable, but that no more makes the seventh-day Sabbath exclusively Jewish than it makes Christmas the exclusive holiday of a family who suddenly decides to start celebrating it. As with the Sabbath, Christmas was there all along—the family just began to take advantage of it.

Directly linked to the Creation account of the seventh day being holy is the fourth commandment of God's law. "Remember the Sabbath day, to keep it holy. Six days you shall labor and do all your work, but the seventh day is the Sabbath of the Lord your God. In it you shall do no work: you, nor your son, nor your daughter, nor your male servant, nor your female servant, nor your cattle, nor your stranger who is within your gates. For in six days the Lord made the heavens and the earth, the sea, and all that is in them, and rested the seventh day. Therefore the Lord blessed the Sabbath day and hallowed it" (Exodus 20:8-11).

Notice how the commandment ties itself directly to the original six-day creation depicted in Genesis. Thus Sabbath, both in the books of Genesis and Exodus, not only links the seventh day to God as Creator, but stresses that He blessed the day and made it holy. Thus the commandment in Exodus isn't teaching the sacredness of the seventh-day Sabbath as a memorial of Creation for the first time. Instead, it is simply telling God's people to "remember" what was already known, that the seventh-day Sabbath was a sacred memorial of Creation, having been blessed and made holy at the end of the Creation week.

THE JOY OF THE SABBATH

Among other things, what God has given to all humanity in the Sabbath is a weekly refuge from the tyranny of time. God *commands* us to rest and to devote one seventh of our lives away from our works. It's not a request, but a stipulation just as much as the prohibitions against murder, adultery, and theft. That's how serious God takes the idea of our weekly rest.

Why? Because He knows that if left to our own, we could never find refuge from the tyrant of time. Time's a hard taskmaster, one that we cannot of ourselves resist. The pull is too strong, the lure too powerful for us to swim against. Hence, God gives us the Sabbath, a refuge from a torrent that would otherwise sweep us away.

> **The Sabbath gives us a block of time every week—and without exception—that we can dedicate in a special way to the ones we love and care about the most.**

So often in the hustle and bustle of life—as we seek to make money, to advance careers, and to get ahead—who gets left behind but spouses, children, and loved ones. God is telling us, *No, I don't want that to happen, and to protect you I have carved out for you this refuge in time, a sacred "place" where the boss, the bills, the things that can dominate you the rest of the week, are not allowed in.*

A wealthy and successful businessman came to the final days of his life. He looked back over the many decades, and as he thought about it, he mused to himself, *If I had to do it all over, I wish I would have spent more time at work and less time with my wife and kids.*

Ridiculous, you say? Who, toward the end of their life, wishes that they had spent less time, not more, with their family and loved ones? Rather, many wish that they had spent less time chasing money and more time with their family. The Sabbath gives us a block of time every week—and without exception—that we can dedicate *in a special way* to the ones we love and care about the most.

A SABBATH FOR ALL THE FAMILY

How interesting, too, that the seventh-day Sabbath is the only institution, along with marriage, that survives from a pre-Fall world. Both existed prior to sin, both come to us from an unfallen world, and both are inherently about relationships. No marriage worth its name can exist without time spent with each other, because only through constant interaction can a relationship deepen and grow. Though certainly a marriage needs more than the Sabbath, the day does provide opportunity for special time together, time that—if protected from the world's weekly distractions—can greatly strengthen the marriage bonds. And in a day and age when marriages are falling apart, how wonderful to have this block of time wrapped in such a special package.

Sabbath isn't just for the spouse, but for the children as well. Especially when they are young, the Sabbath provides special time for them with their parents, because, again, many of the "adult" things— the boss, the job, the bills, the chores—are simply not allowed to intrude, to take away from the time that children want and need with their parents. How many children grow up resentful that their parents were busy with everything in the world but them? The Sabbath can provide an antidote, because, if observed right, it doesn't allow

The Sabbath provides us with the opportunity to build good relationships, and that's because the Sabbath is all about time, and good relationships need time.

"everything in the world" to intrude. Sabbath is no magic bullet. It doesn't guarantee happy close-knit homes. But it does help ensure that families will have the time together that's needed to build those homes, and in our fast-paced world, where the tyranny of time seems to be stronger than ever, what a wonderful refuge.

Whatever all the deep theological ramifications involved (and there are many), the Sabbath provides us with the opportunity to build good relationships, and that's because the Sabbath is all about time, and good relationships need time. Time itself might be eternal, but the amount each of us has isn't. How many precious minutes, weeks, years, decades—forever irrevocably lost to us—have we spent on nothing of value? It's as if someone received millions of dollars in cash and used it as kindling for their fireplace and nothing else. Poet Mark Strand wrote about old people in a nursing home musing over the years of their lives that were now gone. "It is too late to travel/Or even find a reason/To make it seem worthwhile."[11] How sad to look back and not find anything to make our life seem worth it.

PHOTO BY CHALMERS BUTTERFIELD

The elderly often look back in regret about how they have spent their lives.

By partitioning for us a special portion of time *each week*, the Sabbath allows us an opportunity to use this time for what we'll never regret, such as building relationships with those we love and care about. Again, people might regret time wasted on an endless number of things, but who's going to mourn time spent on forging bonds with family and friends? Sabbath gives us that chance by carving out one seventh of our lives that we can use just for that, again allowing nothing to intrude.

THE CREATION

We find, however, much more to this commandment than just building interpersonal relationships.

For starters, if you open *any* Bible, you'll notice that it doesn't begin with a statement about salvation in Jesus, or about the doctrine of justification by faith alone. It doesn't say anything about sin, about judgment, or about the Second Coming.

> By partitioning for us a special portion of time *each week,* the Sabbath allows us an opportunity to use this time for what we'll never regret.

Instead the Bible commences with the doctrine upon which all those other teachings rest, and that's Creation: "In the beginning God created the heavens and the earth" (Genesis 1:1). Creation is the opening act, the first principle, the axiom upon which all else in Scripture follows, because all else becomes meaningless severed from the Lord as Creator.

Think about it. What do the most basic Christians beliefs—salvation, atonement, the cross—mean apart from God as our Creator? What worth is atonement in a godless universe? From what are we saved if God doesn't exist? And if atheistic evolution explains us, then what is the cross but another murdered Jew? How can one make sense of the Fall apart from our origins? After all, what have we fallen from, and to what are we restored? Apart from the biblical account of origins, Christian beliefs—from the cross to the Second Coming—become nonsense.

Another crucial point is that Scripture intricately ties Jesus as Creator with Jesus as Redeemer. John opens his Gospel with words that unmistakably point to Christ the Redeemer as Christ the Creator: "In the beginning was the Word, and the Word was with God, and the Word was God. He was in the beginning with God. All things were made through Him, and without Him nothing was made that was made" (John 1:1-3). Paul, in Colossians, makes a similar point. Speaking about Jesus as Redeemer, he says: "For by Him were all things created that are in heaven and that are on earth, visible and invisible, whether thrones or dominions or principalities or powers. All things were created through Him and for Him" (Colossians 1:16).

> **In Christian theology, Christ's authority, power, and efficacy as the Redeemer arise only from His role as Creator.**

In Christian theology, Christ's authority, power, and efficacy as the Redeemer arise only from His role as Creator. In every sense possible, a major pillar of New Testament theology rests on Jesus as Creator. Christianity, without Christ as the Creator, is a Christianity without Him as Redeemer. And without Christ as Redeemer, Christianity becomes just a variant wing of Judaism, nothing more. We spent the early chapters of this book focusing on Creation because it is so basic to everything that Christianity and the Bible teaches.

SABBATH OR SUNDAY

With Creation, and specifically with Jesus as the Creator, the importance of the seventh-day Sabbath becomes apparent. The seventh-day Sabbath points to Jesus, because He is the Creator, His most basic and fundamental role, the foundation upon which all else that He does rests. He possesses the authority He has because He is the one who "made heaven and earth" (Psalm 124:8; Isaiah 37:16; 2 Chronicles 2:12), and the seventh-day Sabbath is the sign of that authority—one embedded in the creation of "heaven and earth" right from the start.

This becomes important in regard to the question of why most

Christians believe that Sunday, the first day of the week, has replaced the seventh-day Sabbath. At first glance the issue can seem rather unimportant. Why does the specific day—either Sunday, or the day depicted in the fourth commandment itself, the seventh day—really matter? Surely the only important thing is that we have *a* day of rest—*any* day, not which one, right?

Not so fast. If, as we've seen, the *seventh-day* Sabbath is a sign of God's authority, then any alteration of that symbol strikes at the very heart of His authority. The Sabbath-Sunday controversy isn't just about a day—it's about an attempted usurpation by a power that seeks to make itself God, to claim a role that belongs only to Him by virtue of the fact that He, and He alone, is the Creator. To take the specific emblem of His role as Creator, one He instituted Himself, and to replace it with something else represents a flagrant attack against His authority at the most basic level possible.

> **Sundaykeeping, as opposed to Sabbath, is all about a conscious attempt to seize God's ultimate authority as Creator.**

And what many Christians don't know is that this is precisely what Sundaykeeping, as opposed to Sabbath, is all about—a conscious attempt to seize God's ultimate authority as Creator.

WHOM DO WE WORSHIP?

Of course, no one is asserting that most of those who now observe Sunday are seeking to claim God's authority. On the contrary, the overwhelming majority know nothing about what lurked behind the change to Sunday and would be horrified to know the truth. Nor are people who observe Sunday *now*, as opposed to the seventh-day Sabbath, under any kind of divine condemnation.

However, according to the book of Revelation, God is calling people to "worship Him who made heaven and earth, the sea and the springs of water" (Revelation 14:7), that is, to honor Him as Creator (notice, too, how closely linked the language is to that of the fourth commandment in Exodus 20:11: "For in six days the Lord made the heavens and the earth, the sea"). Right along with that call to worship the Lord as Creator is the warning against those who worship the mysterious beast and his image: "If anyone worships the beast and his image, and receives his mark on his forehead or on his hand, he himself shall also drink of the wine of the wrath of God" (Revelation 14:9, 10).

Scripture indicates that in the final days humanity will divide itself into two categories: those who worship God, the Creator, and those who worship the beast and his image (and thus receive the infamous "mark of the beast"). The key element in this separation is *worship*. Either we worship God as our Creator, or we worship the beast and his image. And in the midst of this warning about the beast and the mark of the beast, Revelation describes God's faithful people: "Here is the patience of the saints; here are those who keep *the commandments of God* and the faith of Jesus" (verse 12). They honor and obey God's commandments, and, of all the commandments, only one, the Sabbath, shows why we should worship God—-and that's because He "made the heavens and the earth, the sea, and all that is in them" (Exodus 20:11).

Worship is the key element that will separate humanity into two camps.

We worship God, then, because He and He alone is the Creator, and the Sabbath is the eternal recognition of that Creatorship. Thus, to usurp the seventh day is to strike at the symbol of divine authority. It's an attempt to reach back to Creation week and to undo the institution that He Himself established as an emblem of why we should worship Him as opposed to any other power (such as the beast).

All this becomes even more apparent when one studies how during the early centuries of the Christian church created beings themselves took upon themselves the role of God and instituted a replacement day that had no biblical sanction. The historical evidence is powerful and compelling in regard to how the church in the centuries following the death of Jesus abolished the observance of the seventh-day Sabbath, replacing it with Sunday. Paul warned about a power that would seek to usurp the role of God Himself: "Don't

> Paul warned about a power that would seek to usurp the role of God Himself.

let anyone deceive you in any way, for that day will not come until the rebellion occurs and the man of lawlessness is revealed, the man doomed to destruction. He will oppose and will exalt himself over everything that is called God or is worshiped, so that he sets himself up in God's temple, proclaiming himself to be God" (2 Thessalonians 2:3, 4, NIV). This has already happened, and a lot more subtly than Paul's strident language could leave someone, reading superficially, to believe.

In short, because Sabbath is the symbol of God's authority as Creator, and Sunday is a human institution that attempts to usurp that authority; and because the issue in the last days will be over whether we worship God, the Creator, or the beast (a human institution) and his image; and because Scripture describes God's faithful people as those who honor the commandments of God, which includes the seventh-day Sabbath—many Christians believe that the Sabbath-Sunday debate will eventually unfurl into an issue with tremendous spiritual and eternal consequences. If the seventh-day Sabbath is a sign of His creative authority, it's not hard to see why Sunday, which without divine sanction has all but replaced that day in Christendom, will become associated with the mark of the beast.

LEGALISTS?

One final point worth considering: Those who honor the seventh-day Sabbath often get accused of legalism, of trying to work their way to heaven. Yet how is it that the one commandment devoted to rest has been turned into the universal symbol of salvation by human effort?

What's wrong with this picture?

Far from being a metaphor of works, the Sabbath is the Bible's most fundamental symbol of the rest that God's people have always had in Him. From the pre-Fall world of Adam and Eve's Eden to the New Covenant rest that God's followers have in Christ's work of redemption for them ("There remains therefore a rest for the people of God" [Hebrews 4:9]), the Sabbath is a real-time manifestation of the rest that Christ offers to all (Matthew 11:28).

Anyone can say that they are resting in Christ and are saved by grace. But the honoring of the seventh-day Sabbath is a visible expression of that rest, a living parable of what it means to be covered by His grace. Weekly rest from secular, worldly works stands as a symbol of the rest that Jesus gives His people through His completed work of salvation. "For he who has entered His rest has himself also ceased from his own works as God did from His" (Hebrews 4:10). Obedience to this commandment is a way of saying: "Hey, we're so sure of our salvation in Jesus, we're so firm and secure in what Christ has done for us, that we can—in a special way—rest from any of our works, because we know what Christ has accomplished for humanity through His death and resurrection."

> The irony of it all is that by resting, people get accused of trying to work their way to heaven.

It would seem that by firmly adhering to the commandments against adultery, stealing, covetousness, or idolatry, people could be accused, at least a little more logically and reasonably, of legalism, of salvation by works (that is, if one could be charged with legalism for obeying any of the commandments). But is anyone trying to work their way to heaven because they rest on the seventh-day Sabbath?

The irony of it all is that by resting, people get accused of trying to work their way to heaven—an argument that makes about as much sense as a parricide pleading for mercy because he's an orphan.

_____

[1] Leo Tolstoy, "The Story of Ivan the Fool," *Walk in the Light and Twenty-three Tales* (Maryknoll, N.Y.: Orbis Books, 2003), p. 206.

[2] *Ibid.*, p. 235.

[3] Excerpted in *Harper's Magazine,* August 2004, p. 14.

[4] See Act I, scene 2, lines 97-131.

[5] Leo Tolstoy, "How Much Land Does a Man Need?" *The Kreutzer Sonata and Other Short Stories* (Mineola, N.Y.: Dover Publications, 1993), p. 2.

[6] *Ibid.*

[7] *Ibid.*, p. 9.

[8] *Ibid.*

[9] *Ibid.*, p. 14.

[10] *Ibid.*

[11] Mark Strand, "Old People on the Nursing Home Porch," *Selected Poems* (New York: Alfred A. Knopf, 2004), p. 8.

[12] The following quotes help explain the background to the change of the seventh-day Sabbath to the first day. "Now in the matter of the Sabbath observance the Protestant rule of faith is utterly unable to explain the substitution of the Christian Sunday for the Jewish Saturday. It has been changed. The Bible still teaches that the Sabbath or Saturday should be kept holy. There is no authority in the New Testament for the substitution of Sunday for Saturday. Surely it is an important matter. It stands there in the Bible as one of the Ten Commandments of God. There is no authority in the Bible for abrogating this commandment, or for transferring its observance to another day of the week.

"For Catholics it is not the slightest difficulty. 'All power is given Me in heaven and on earth; as the Father sent Me so I also send you,' said our Divine Lord in giving tremendous commission to His apostles. 'He that heareth you heareth Me.'" We have in the authoritative voice of the Church the voice of Christ Himself. The Church is above the Bible; and this transference of Sabbath observance from Saturday to Sunday is proof positive of that fact. Deny the authority of the Church and you have no adequate or reasonable explanation or justification for the substitution of Sunday for Saturday" (*The Catholic Record*, Sept. 1, 1923).

"Q. Have you any other way of proving that the [Roman Catholic] Church has the power to institute festivals of precept?"

"A. Had she not such power, she could not have done that in which all modern religionists agree with her;—she could not have substituted the observance of Sunday, the first day of the week, for the observance of Saturday, the seventh day of the week, a change for which there is no Scriptural authority" (Stephan Keenan, *A Doctrinal Catechism*, 3rd American ed., rev. [New York: T. W. Strong, late Edward Dunigan & Bro., 1876], p. 174).

FAMILY MATTERS

THE SECOND TABLET

any often depict the Ten Commandments in two divisions: the first four on one tablet, the last six on another, possibly because of length (the second and fourth commandments are quite long). At the same time, though, it also recognizes that the first four commandments deal specifically with our relationship to God, while the last six focus on our relationship to other people. The first section is heavenly-orientated, the second more earthly.

However convenient, the break is in many

The last six commandments deal with our human relationships.

ways artificial. As the previous chapter has shown, the first four commandments, whatever their distinct spiritual/theological emphasis, greatly influence the practical and relational elements of human life, and that's because our relationship to God directly shapes our relationship to others. "By this we know love, because He laid down His life for us. And we also ought to lay down our lives for the brethren. But whoever has this world's goods, and sees his brother in need, and shuts up his heart from him, how does the love of God abide in him? My little children, let us not love in word or in tongue, but in deed and in truth" (1 John 3:16-18).

THE FIFTH COMMANDMENT

Nevertheless, there does seem to be a dramatic shift from the Sabbath commandment to the next one, which reads: "Honor your father and your mother, that your days may be long upon the land which the Lord your God is giving you" (Exodus 20:12).

Yet it's not so radical. The Sabbath functions as a bridge between those commandments oriented toward God and heaven (we rest on the seventh day because God did) and yet is earthly-orientated as well, because it gives us a rest that opens the way for deepening our personal relationships with others (including parents). Also, the fourth commandment points to God as our Creator. The only ones coming even close to that role are, of course, our parents, the focus of the next commandment. Hence, the flow from the Sabbath to the commandment to honor our parents is a logical one.

Though given in a totally different context than today, and in a world radically different from ours, the principle behind the fifth commandment remains just as valid now as at Mount Sinai. No human being exists independent of his or her parents. Regardless of the kind of relationship we have with our parents now or even what kind of parents they are (whether worthy of honor or respect), they are still our parents—our creators, *as it were*—and from that fact alone they should receive at least *some* honor.

THE MOST NATURAL COMMANDMENT

At first glance the fifth commandment seems strangely redundant. Don't *most* people, in *most* situations, *love* their mother and father? Why, then, command them to do what's about as natural as breathing? An injunction merely to honor parents—when in most cases people love them—seems about as strange as ordering someone, dying of thirst, to lick the condensation off the side of a tall cool glass of ice-cold water when most likely what they will really do, if left alone, is drink the whole glass!

Why command what's natural?

It's because we're in a world so steeped in sin that the natural has become perverted and distorted to the point that not everyone is inclined to do what would be at a minimum the most obvious thing in the world to do. For example, try forcing a 12-year-old girl to love a father who sexually assaulted her and gave her AIDS (honoring the father would be hard enough). Or consider telling the boy whose father beat him into a coma with a baseball bat that he should love his father (again, honoring him would be hard enough). That's why the command tells us to honor our parents. It doesn't order us to feel love for them, because God knew that some people wouldn't, couldn't, or maybe even shouldn't love their parents in the normal way.

> "I didn't get along with their mothers, so why should I have gotten along with the kids?"

What this commandment is saying to us, basically, is that the family unit is the foundation of all human society, and that we need to hold it intact the best we can, whatever the circumstances. Even after the children are grown and gone, family bonds remain vital, and by honoring our parents we are acknowledging links and helping keep them intact. This is important, because in the end the key to our happiness often lies in our relationships, especially family ones.

Who hasn't read about famous people who have everything the world could offer, and yet remain miserable? And what, almost always, is the cause of their unhappiness? It's not poverty, obscurity, or poor health. In almost every case it's always the same thing—bad family relationships.

Band leader Artie Shaw had been married to some of Hollywood's most glamorous sex goddesses. At the end of his life, talking about the bad relationships he had not only with these women but with the children he had sired with them, he said, "I didn't get along with their mothers, so why should I have gotten along with the kids?" Image all the pain that these bad relationships caused, and who knows for how many generations and in what various forms that pain will continue.

Artie Shaw

PUBLIC DOMAIN

God originally created us to be a family: mothers, fathers, children. And that's why the Ten Commandments are so family-orientated. They seek to protect family relationships. And by doing that, the commandments help ensure our own personal happiness. Sure, a good close-knit loving family doesn't guarantee happiness, but it's hard to think of anything more likely to bring it.

RECIPROCAL

In the New Testament the apostle Paul expounds and expands on the commandment about honoring parents: "Children, obey your parents in the Lord, for this is right. 'Honor your father and mother,' which is the first commandment with promise: 'that it may be well with you and you may live long on the earth.' And you, fathers, do not provoke your children to wrath, but bring them up in the training and admonition of the Lord" (Ephesians 6:1-4).

> How you relate to your children when they're young will greatly shape how they respond to you when they are older.

His emphasis is on the children—on what they are to do. Obey your parents, he urges, and honor them. He also repeats, in his own words, the rest of the commandment, which stresses that good things will happen if they do honor their parents, the idea being that it is a crucial key to happiness, to stability, to a good family life, and to good family relations. God has given us a command to help protect that family life. In other words, as we've been saying all through *Life Without Limits*, what we do has consequences here and now, either for good or for evil.

But after discussing the fifth commandment and the duty of children to parents, Paul then switches to parents, particularly the father, and tells them not to antagonize their children but to bring them up in a healthy relationship to God. Sure, we're commanded to honor our mother and father, regardless of what kind of parent they are. But how much easier that would be were parents to do what Paul said: not to provoke their children, but to love them, to treat them with respect, to give them the kind of life that could make it easy for them, when they are adults, to honor them?

Imagine how much better our homes, families, and lives would be were all parents to love, nurture, and treat their children well, and the children, in response, did the same thing to their parents all their lives. What a better, happier world it would be, right?

It's reciprocal. How you relate to your children when they're young will greatly shape how they respond to you when they are older. How many wretched, dysfunctional families have ruined the lives of millions, passing their misery from one generation to another, all because parents treated their children badly, and the children reacted in the same way? This commandment, if kept, would go a long way in helping break this vicious, never-ending cycle of suffering and woe.

THE NEAREST 10 MILLION

We can begin looking at the sixth commandment ("You shall not murder") with one of the more high-profile murders, such as the Charles Manson gang, which in 1969 entered the mansion of actress Sharon Tate, then pregnant, and stabbed her and four other victims about 100 times, killing them all.

Or we could use the sensational case of Richard Speck, who stunned the world in 1966 after sexually assaulting and then slaying eight nurses in a single night.

And who can forget the murder and cannibalism committed by young Jeffrey Dahmer?

If one isn't interested in such headline gore, we can always turn to the more routine types that we read about, pretty much daily, in most big-city newspapers anywhere in the world. One drug dealer kills another drug dealer. A husband murders his wife, or a wife shoots her husband. A gang member assassinates a rival gang member. It's so common anymore that it's usually buried somewhere deep in the paper, often on the same page as mortgage ads.

Of course, these are just individual murders. One murder here, four there, six somewhere else, eight in a distant city . . . small stuff. History provides the really big numbers. The Rwanda genocide, the Holocaust, the Chinese Cultural Revolution, Stalin's atrocities—the list goes on and on, and that's just the recent past.

"In this century," Richard John Neuhaus commented during the 1990s, "so many people have been deliberately killed by other people that the estimates of historians vary by the tens of millions, and they end up by agreeing to split the difference or to round off the victim count at the nearest ten million."[1]

> So damaged by sin, we have to be commanded to do what should come naturally, and we have to be forbidden to do what should be unnatural.

How painfully ironic that the commandment against killing comes right after the one to honor parents. The fifth commandment would, as we said, seem the most natural thing to do, and yet God directs us *to do* it, while committing murder would seem to be the most unnatural thing to do, and we *are forbidden to do* it. Again, so damaged by sin, we have to be commanded to do what should come naturally, and we have to be forbidden to do what should be unnatural.

YOU SHALL NOT KILL

Most people, whatever their beliefs, understand the rationale and reason behind the sixth commandment. No family, community, or society would survive were not this prohibition understood, even intuitively, and then implemented.

Yet Jesus does something remarkable with this commandment:

"You have heard that it was said to the people long ago, 'Do not murder, and anyone who murders will be subject to judgment.' But I tell you that anyone who is angry with his brother will be subject to judgment. Again, anyone who says to his brother, 'Raca,' is answerable to the Sanhedrin. But anyone who says, 'You fool!' will be in danger of the fire of hell.

"Therefore, if you are offering your gift at the altar and there remember that your brother has something against you, leave your gift there in front of the altar. First go and be reconciled to your brother; then come and offer your gift.

"Settle matters quickly with your adversary who is taking you to court. Do it while you are still with him on the way, or he may hand you over to the judge, and the judge may hand you over to the officer, and you may be thrown into prison. I tell you the truth, you will not get out until you have paid the last penny" (Matthew 5:21-26, NIV).

Whatever the immediate cultural issues Jesus addressed here, the

Settling matters with our adversaries can save us from prison.

> Jesus is telling us to uproot, early, the mentality that can lead to the horrific consequences that always follow murder. He turned a commandment about murder into one about forgiveness, reconciliation, and healing, making it as much for the "murderer" as for the "murdered."

principle is universal—and astounding. One doesn't need Moses, or Christian morality, to know that murder is wrong. Jesus, however, pulls the commandment back from the extremes of taking a life and applies it to the thoughts and emotions that often precede the act itself. He radicalizes the obvious. Everyone knows murder is wrong. But to equate murder with thoughts, feelings, or words? Why?

It's easy. Imagine if people dealt with anger before it expanded into violence? Jesus is telling us to uproot, early, the mentality that can lead to the horrific consequences that always follow murder. He turned a commandment about murder into one about forgiveness, reconciliation, and healing, making it as much for the "murderer" as for the "murdered." Christ wants to spare us the bitterness, the hatred, the suffering that comes from harboring the kind of sentiments that could—if pushed—kill. You don't have to pull the trigger in order for your life to be marred, even ruined, by the desire that could lead you to pull it.

MURDER IN HIS HEART

Years ago an American soldier who fought in Vietnam came back injured. Paul Reed seethed with so much anger and hatred against the Communists that he was an emotional wreck (no purple hearts are given out for that kind of injury, though).

One day, bored, he opened a box that he had brought from Vietnam but had never opened. Among its contents was a small book filled with the writings of a North Vietnamese soldier whom he had killed. Impressed by the handwriting, Paul—for some reason—had it translated. Stunned by the beauty and sensitivity of what he read, he for the first time saw the humanity of the man that he had hated so bitterly. Nothing he had read,

Forgiveness can heal even the horrors of war.

though, affected him more than these words written by this North Vietnamese Communist solider: "Forget about everything. Calm yourself. Love bears no grudge."

Suddenly, the Vietnamese whom he had for years viewed as nothing but animals became human. His true enemy wasn't Communists. Rather, he now realized, it was the hatred that boiled his organs inside his own flesh. Paul Reed suddenly recognized that he was violating the commandment against murder, except that the person he was killing was himself.

Though thinking he would fail, Paul—for his own good—wanted to find the family of the man whom he had killed, and give them back the book. After a lot of searching and inquiry, he discovered that the soldier, Nguyen van Nghia, had not died but, severely injured, made it back home in the north. Reed determined to meet him and return the book.

After so many years of murder and hatred in his heart, Paul Reed went to Vietnam, located Nguyen, and handed him the diary. The men stood before each other.

"Nguyen," Paul said, "can you forgive me?"

"Yes, I do," his former enemy answered. "And do you forgive me?"

Tears in his eyes, Paul said, "Yes."

Reed left Vietnam cured of the injury that he had first got there—the hatred in his heart that had ruined him emotionally. But what about Nguyen's injury, which had scarred his face and left him almost blind? With the help of other Vietnam veterans, Paul had Nguyen van Nghia brought to the United States. Doctors examined him, and although surgery could do nothing to help, they fitted him with a special pair of glasses that enabled him to see clearly at least out of one eye.

Paul had closed the circle, at least as far it could be done in such a fallen world as ours.

> Most people don't have to worry about committing physical murder, but they do have to struggle with anger, bitterness, and resentment, things that can ruin their lives by causing them to commit murder in their heart and, if nothing else, slaughter their own soul.

DELIVERANCE FROM THE DEMON OF HATE

Of course, Paul's experience was only an isolated case. But that's the point. All the world's hatred is nothing but a vast conglomeration of isolated cases. Hatred is always committed only by individuals who—whether in groups or alone—choose to hate. And so, whether together or in isolation, they could, one by one, make the decision (by obeying the sixth commandment as Jesus told us to) to be freed of that demon.

Jesus took a commandment meant for potential murderers and applied it to every human being—to mothers, fathers, sisters, brothers, friends, neighbors—and with it offering them the key to healing, peace, and reconciliation. Most people don't have to worry about committing physical murder, but they do have to struggle with anger, bitterness, and resentment, things that can ruin their lives by causing them to commit murder in their heart and, if nothing else, slaughter their own soul.

But this commandment, interpreted through Christ's words, offers us something so much better. Life's too short to let hatred, bitterness, and anger consume it. Jesus urges us to come to Him so that He can offer us a way out. How much better our families and all our relationships would be were we to take this to heart. You can't change others who themselves might seethe with anger and bitterness. But you don't have to—you need, instead, to deal with your soul, the one you're going to have to answer for.

Richard Nixon

Whatever one might think of him or his place in history, former American president Richard Nixon, when resigning the White House after the Watergate scandal, caught the essence of what Jesus meant. Standing before the White House staff just before his departure, Nixon said: "Always remember, others may hate you, but those who hate you don't win unless you hate them, and then you destroy yourself."

That's the essence of the sixth commandment.

THIS RATHER IMPLAUSIBLE PROCESS

If human sexuality isn't proof of evolution's inadequacy to explain our origins, what is? We are supposed to believe that—through undirected processes, with no conscious goal or purpose—male and female sex organs evolved by chance into what they are today? Even if one were to accept such a proposal, is it not reasonable to ask, *How did humans (or even any lower mammalians that breed as mammals do) procreate for the millions of years it is presumed to have taken for the male and female sex organs and processes and instincts to finally evolve in order that procreation could take place?* It must have required an untold number of generations, but how did those generations get there when all the incredibly complicated mechanisms needed for that to happen did not yet exist? Let's say that female sexuality (womb, sex organs, emotional drives, ovulation, lactation) evolved a few million years before the man's (or vice versa). How did organisms keep reproducing when the very process by which they were created hadn't yet emerged into being? All the sperms cells in the world can't, without an egg, make a baby; nor all the eggs, without sperm. *And yet somehow all this came together, by pure chance alone?* (And people think Christianity is unreasonable?)

No doubt, endless Ph.D. theses and so forth have speculated on how this might have happened, but that's all it can be—speculation—because no one has seen any such process unfold.

EVIDENCE FOR A LOVING DEITY

In contrast, besides being a strong argument against evolution, human sexuality is powerful evidence not only for God but for a loving deity, one who created humans with the potential for almost unbelievable physical ecstasy. If He had intended sex for procreation alone, He could have

> Human sexuality is powerful evidence not only for God but for a loving deity, one who created humans with the potential for almost unbelievable physical ecstasy.

created some other mechanism by which a man could fertilize a woman's egg and a baby be born, all without anywhere near the physical pleasure that human sexuality allows for. (God could have made it feel no better than letting out a good belch and humans would still do it.) And then, beyond just procreation, add the level of intimacy, passion, and love that sex can express for human beings, and we encounter powerful proof for God that all the speculating and theorizing and philosophizing just can't touch.

If we remember Clifford's principle ("It is always wrong, everywhere and for anyone, to believe anything upon insufficient evidence"), what's more logical and reasonable to believe: that human sexuality arose purely by chance through undirected processes that through time just happened to create sex organs, wombs, ovulation, and passion, or that a loving Creator who wanted human beings to enjoy their bodies put all the nerves, organs, and processes in place in order for them to enjoy a physical intimacy and ecstasy that can leave them, literally, moaning and screaming in pleasure?

THE GIFT

Picture the following: a father leaves his son an inheritance of fabulous wealth. The potential for good is enormous if the son follows the basic principles that the father set down, knowing that any violation of them would lead his son to ruin because the gift itself is so powerful. The son, rejecting those principles, uses the money to indulge in his own pleasures, passions, and selfish desires. Instead of the wealth creating good in ways that the son could never have imagined, it produces misery not only for him but for endless others. How tragic, when the gift in and of itself was so full of the potential for good.

The analogy's obvious. If ever humans needed evidence of God's love for them, the gift of sex is it. And yet, if ever there were an abused gift, one meant for good that has turned out to be the cause of so much human disaster, the gift of sex is it, too.

Yet it didn't have to be this way. God set down one simple basic rule, one commandment, that if followed could have spared teeming

Sex outside of marriage has ruined countless lives.

millions so much suffering and pain. It's the seventh commandment: "You shall not commit adultery" (Exodus 20:14).

What numbers, what charts, or what formulas can measure the rage, the pain, and the damage caused by violation of this commandment? How many childhoods, homes, marriages, and lives has sex outside of the boundaries that God has created for it (sex between one man married to one woman) eventually destroyed?

Sounds prudish? old-fashioned? narrow?

Ask any of the millions of children who had their homes shattered by an adulterous parent if the commandment is so prudish. Would the millions suffering with sexually transmitted disease caught through sex outside of marriage, especially those women made barren from the disease, consider the commandment old-fashioned? More millions of unwed girls who became pregnant as teenagers now wish that they had obeyed it. And those dying of AIDS caught through sex outside of marriage would not regard the commandment as too narrow.

In 1970, at the height of the "sexual revolution," *Life* magazine had an article that said: "In the first place, we must rid our minds of the idea that there are any special moral rules for sexual behavior. Sexual pleasure is never wrong."

Never wrong? Outside of marriage between a husband and a wife, it's always wrong—and millions of ruined lives prove it.

God gave human beings sex as a gift, and, in the right context, they are to enjoy that gift—a lot, even! Here's what the New Testament says about sex between a husband and a wife: "But since there is so much immorality, each man should have his own wife, and each woman her own husband. The husband should fulfill his marital duty to his wife, and likewise the wife to her husband. The wife's body does not belong to her alone but also to her husband. In the same way, the husband's body does not belong to him alone but also to his wife. Do not deprive each other except by mutual consent and for a time, so that you may devote yourselves to prayer. Then come together again so that Satan will not tempt you because of your lack of self-control" (1 Corinthians 7:2, NIV).

The New Testament tells married couples, basically, not to deprive each other of sexual love. The only thing it warns against in regard to sex is abstinence from it! The Bible isn't prudish about sex. On the contrary, God wants humanity to enjoy it to the fullest potential possible, and nothing can destroy that more than adultery or sex outside of the security of a marriage.

REMORSE, SCANDAL, HATRED

Discussing the seventh commandment, Jesus interpreted its broader implications. "You have heard that it was said to those of old, 'You shall not commit adultery.' But I say to you that whoever looks at a woman to lust for her has already committed adultery with her in his heart" (Matthew 5:27, 28).

Why so blunt? Because Jesus knows just how powerful the human sex drive is (not only did He create it but, as a human, He experienced it) and just how devastating its abuse can be. He was warning people, especially men (who have a much harder time controlling it, as a rule, than do women), to deal with it at the first level it arises— in the heart and mind. Grapple with it then, where it's much easier to control. Stop the surge of passion before it destroys you and your loved ones.

God created sex, like the family, to give us the maximum good, pleasure, and fulfillment in life. Yet all that potential, if unleashed in the wrong direction, will cause the maximum misery and suffering instead. Adolf Hitler was one of the previous century's most power-

God created sex, like the family, to give us the maximum good, pleasure, and fulfillment in life.

ful orators. Think about how much suffering would have been allevi-
ated had he used his oratorical gifts the way Billy Graham did his.

Author and poet Delmore Schwartz wrote a short story about a
young man dreaming that he was in a movie theater in which his
father's courtship of his mother played across the screen. At one point
the young man jumped up and shouted: "Don't do it. It's not too late
to change your minds, both of you. Nothing good will come of it,
only remorse, hatred, scandal and two children whose characters are
monstrous."[2]

Though only fiction, his words revealed the family life and childhood that Delmore and his brother suffered through after the
breakup of his parents' marriage because of his dad's adultery. This
family tragedy haunted Delmore
for the rest of his life, which at 53
ended in alcoholism, insanity, and
poverty—a lonely death in a sleazy
New York hotel for a man who
never got over the trauma of his
early family life.

> When done right, the family creates the best that humanity offers.

The home was meant to be a
fortress, a bastion of love, security,
and trust, not a font of remorse, hatred, and scandal. When done right,
the family creates the best that humanity offers, but when it's abused or
its sacred boundaries are violated, it drags us to the dregs. Who doesn't
cringe at accounts of how low some families have gone, if for no other
reason than it's the one place humanity should be brought so high?

And though many forces can ruin or hurt a family, nothing is
more perfectly calibrated than adultery. A fire can consume your
house, but nothing else can destroy a home like adultery.

That's why Jesus spoke so strongly against it.

THE FALL

Young Jeff was smarter than everyone else. Just ask him. He grad-
uated near the top of not only his high school class, but of Harvard

Business School as well (MBA, 1979). Within 12 years, and to no one's surprise (certainly not his own), he had become CEO (chief executive officer) and board chair of one the biggest companies in the world. It ranked number 7 on the Fortune 500 list, claiming $101 billion in annual revenues. And Jeff was still in his 40s.

Jeff, of course, was highly compensated, making millions of dollars in bonuses (that is, above a $14 million yearly salary), including one year in which he pulled in $132 million, all of which fueled a nice lifestyle: mansions, expensive trips to Europe, motorcycle rides in the Mexican desert, scavenger hunts in the Australian outback. You name it, and if Jeffrey wanted it, he got it. After all, didn't he deserve it, being as smart and as talented as he was?

Without question, he had reached the pinnacle of success, if you define it as money, power, influence, and prestige.

Unfortunately, he had one slight problem. He was a thief, enriching himself and his cronies at the expense of his own company, Enron, which eventually collapsed in the second-largest bankruptcy in United States history, costing thousands of workers their jobs and pension plans.

Though Jeffrey Skilling brashly testified before Congress about his innocence, he was found guilty in 2006 of fraud (after spending tens of millions on lawyers) and sentenced to more than 24 years in prison, which for a man at 52 was pretty much the rest of his life.

Of course, as tragic as the Skilling story is (he will now make, in prison, about 12 cents to $1.25 an hour, depending on what he does), we should save our tears for many of the 20,000 former Enron employees who lost their life savings when the company went belly-up in 2001, especially because most of their pension plans had been heavily invested in Enron stock. When the stock started falling, company executives didn't allow them to sell their shares, even though

Greed creates financial disaster.

they—Skilling and others—were dumping theirs like crazy. As the company he oversaw collapsed, Jeffrey reaped millions of dollars (at one point selling $60 million worth of stock) while thousands of employees—who believed management's words that the company was doing fine—watched their pension plans vanish as Enron stock plummeted from a high of $90 a share to less than $1.

People whose retirement portfolios had about as much in them as what Skilling made in about two months were now left with nothing—no job, no health insurance, no pension.

Diana Peters was one. During Thanksgiving week 2001, when rumors circulated about the company's trouble (despite denials by the executives), her husband was diagnosed with inoperable brain cancer. The following Monday she went to work at Enron, where her supervisor announced that everyone had 30 minutes to collect their personal belongings and leave, because they no longer had jobs. By 9:00 a.m. she had no job, no health insurance, and a husband with a brain tumor, not to mention the loss of $75,000 in retirement savings, probably what Jeffrey spent on some of his vacations.

Though Medicare and Social Security helped her cover her husband's medical expenses, she was forced to find temporary work, cleaning offices with her son on weekends just to survive. All this while Skilling and his cohorts milked the company for hundreds of millions!

Multiply that story by thousands of others, some even worse, and one understands the tragedy of Enron.

THE EIGHTH COMMANDMENT

Of course, who needs Moses, or even Jesus, to know the truth of the words: "You shall not steal" (Exodus 20:15)? No one, not even a thief, likes to be robbed. Yet all over the world prisons teem with those who have violated that commandment (and those are only the ones who got caught).

Now, not all theft comes with the vast consequences of Enron, which ruined the lives, not just of the thieves and their immediate

Today we have to protect even our computers from thievery.

©ISTOCKPHOTO.COM/JOXXXXJO

families, but thousands of others as well. Yet thievery doesn't have to be so extensive to have terrible results. It's not just the loss of material goods, as bad as that can be—it's the sense of outrage, violation, and injustice that's suffered by the victim. An aura of "sacredness" exists around ownership, around the idea of something being your own. Whether it involves a piece or land or a piece of candy, ownership is natural, basic to humanity, and when that's violated—be it through corporate fraud or the slyness of a pickpocket—our basic humanity itself feels defiled as well. No wonder all human beings react so strongly against it.

But it's not just what stealing does to the victim (that's obvious); it's also what it does to the thief, even if never detected. Who needs a written law to know that robbery is wrong? It's etched in our conscience. And then, add to that what society and God's law says, and people steal only through ignoring that conscience. Yet with each violation the etching gets sanded down until it's smoothed over under a pack of slick justifications and rationalizations that never quite quell the inner nagging.

What's worse, becoming used to quelling (or at least trying to quell) the conscience in one area, people find it easier to disregard it in others, and before long they're boldly doing things that would have once horrified them. And as we've already seen, our immoral actions affect others, especially those closest to us.

Without question, if someone is stealing, other sins probably aren't far behind. Thank goodness for the gospel, then. It offers the hope and prospect not just of forgiveness but of restoration. Salvation is for the thief, too.

> If someone is stealing, other sins probably aren't far behind. The gospel offers the hope and prospect not just of forgiveness but of restoration. Salvation is for the thief, too.

In Victor Hugo's *Les Misérables* Jean Valjean, a bitter and hateful thief, experiences the power of forgiveness and redemption. That's the good news of the gospel. Regardless of your past, whether a Jeffrey Skilling or a pickpocket, not only can God forgive you, but He can restore you, making you whole and honest as well.

PUBLIC DOMAIN

Victor Hugo

"Therefore, if anyone is in Christ, he is a new creation; the old has gone, the new has come!" (2 Corinthians 5:17, NIV).

The commandment "You shall not steal" isn't a magical remedy for sin. You'll find no more of a cure there than you will find on the chart in which the doctor writes down the symptoms of your disease. The commandment merely points to the problem.

The solution is Jesus.

Machiavelli's *Mandragola*

Almost five centuries ago Niccolò Machiavelli wrote a comedy called *Mandragola* about a liar and schemer named Callimaco. Wanting to seduce another man's wife (known for her faithfulness), Callimaco enlists the help of a marriage broker named Ligurio, who devises a plan in which the wife, unable to have children, receives a potion that (she's promised) will enable her to. The only problem (she's told) is that the potion, a special kind of poison, will kill the first person who sleeps with her after she drinks it, and she certainly doesn't want that to be her husband, so she is going to have to find a temporary lover. (Guess who that is?) The ploy works, and, though endless machinations and deceit, Callimaco achieves his goal.

What's fascinating about the play is that none of the characters can succeed in their desires without lies and deception. Even the "innocent" get caught up in it, including Friar Timoteo, who—after Ligurio

Niccolò Machiavelli

offers him cash (supposedly to help the poor)—finally agrees to play his role.

"Now I see," Ligurio tells the friar, "that you are truly the religious man I took you for."[3]

When the play ends, all the characters—through lying, cheating, and deceiving—have gotten what they wanted. Machiavelli's point is that lying and deception are fine if they allow one to achieve one's goals. For him, the ends, whatever they may be, justify the means, whatever they are.

And why not? After all, think about it. Throughout this book we have explored two contrasting—and conflicting—concepts of reality: a secular atheistic view in which our existence arose from pure chance, the accidental assembling of atoms that through a vicious yet purposeless process of evolution created a humanity that's doomed to eternal extinction by the same cold uncaring forces that first brought it here. Or its polar opposite, that we're the purposeful product of a God who planned our existence, who loves us, who established a moral order in the world, and who offers us the hope of eternal life.

Now, if the first is true, that we are the products of the confluence of accidental forces, and that through a vicious and predatory "survival of the fittest" cycle of violence the stronger, smarter, better adapted triumphed at the expense of the weaker—then what's wrong with lying or deception if that helps one endure or even thrive? Far from being immoral, lying in order to advance yourself, even to the detriment of others (or *especially* at the detriment of others), would seem consonant with natural laws themselves.

In contrast, the essence of Christian virtue, that of self-denial and self-sacrifice for the good of others, would be in opposition to the laws of nature. And so would the ninth commandment of God's law ("You shall not bear false witness against your neighbor" [Exodus 20:16]), especially when "bearing false witness" would be to your own personal advantage, regardless of what that deception did to your neighbor. In the evolu-

> We're moral beings in a moral world created by a moral God. No matter how worn down, even at the genetic level by thousands of years of sin, our moral compunction is still there, still wired in us.

tionary model, if lying advances you at the expense of someone else, it would be the *only* right thing to do.

GUILTY CONSCIENCE

Why, though, does almost everyone, even those who don't believe in, know about, or care about the ninth commandment, suffer everything from a twinge of guilt to a squeezing oppression when they lie? Why do most people intuitively sense that lying is wrong? How is it that atheistic evolutionists intuit that lying isn't right even when it will aid their own advancement? And why do they feel that something is amiss when, according to their own model of origins, lying is merely another expression of the forces that create us to begin with?

It's because we're moral beings in a moral world created by a moral God, that's why. No matter how worn down, even at the genetic level, by thousands of years of sin, our moral compunction is still there, still wired in us. And though the practice of any wrong action through time all but neutralizes our inner resistance to it, the fact that it was there to begin with testifies to its reality, no matter how far many have run from it.

Notice, too, that all the other commandments so far have dealt only with actions. The ninth commandment is the only one devoted to our words, to our speech. It's taking morality to another level, a deeper one, because if we will obey God here, we will obey in others as well. Someone unwilling to lie isn't likely to steal, to kill, or to commit adultery, either. People rarely commit one sin. Those who steal lie, those who kill lie, and those who commit adultery lie. They have to. In contrast, how many who don't lie will steal, kill, or indulge in adultery? If someone can surrender themselves to the Lord at the level of their words, if they are committed to Him to the

Most people sense that truth and lies follow totally separate paths.

> We don't need to believe in Jesus to recognize that we shouldn't lie. What we need Him for is to have the power not to, even when the temptation is great.

point at which they will not, through His power, lie—then what are the chances of them breaking other commandments?

And, as we've seen, how much better, healthier, happier our lives, families, and communities would be were everyone to obey those divine laws?

Sure, we don't need to believe in Jesus to recognize that we shouldn't lie. What we need Him for is to have the power not to, even when the temptation is great, the immediate rewards seem plentiful, and moral motivation inside us—jerked and stretched flaccid—is no longer enough to keep us from doing what we know is wrong.

ORWELL'S NIGHTMARE

Reality TV began not with *Survivor* but with *Candid Camera*, in which the producers placed unsuspecting people in confusing, embarrassing, or hilarious situations as a hidden camera filmed their reactions. Pranks included vending machines that talked, hands that popped out of mailboxes and grabbed mail, ridiculously small portions of food served in restaurants, and hundreds of other tricks played on unwitting participants who walked into these strange situations (imagine the look on the face of some guy who entered an office for some business reason only to find the secretary chained to her desk) and had no idea about what was happening until someone stepped onto the scene and uttered the famous words "Smile; you're on *Candid Camera!*"

While most of us never had a cameo appearance on *Candid Camera*, we all surely get recorded without our knowledge. Walk into almost any public building, from a bank to a convenience store, and your every move is likely to be digitized. In most larger Western cities you can't stroll down the street without cameras recording your actions, a fact that has helped solve numerous crimes simply because the culprits got filmed committing them.

Of course, it's one thing to be recorded in public and quite another to be watched in the privacy of your own residence. Yet in George Orwell's novel *1984* he depicted a future world (he wrote it in 1948) in which everyone was under the constant scrutiny of the ubiquitous Thought Police, even in their own homes.

"There was of course," he wrote, "no way of knowing whether you were being watched at any given moment. . . . It was even conceivable that they watched everybody all the time. But at any rate they could plug in your wire whenever they wanted to. You had to live— did live, from habit that became instinct—in the assumption that every sound you made was overheard, and, except in darkness, every movement scrutinized."[4]

Even worse, the government watched everything so closely that it punished even wrong thoughts. Called "Thought Crime," those caught in it faced punishment (i.e., torture and death).

"Whether he wrote DOWN WITH BIG BROTHER, or whether he refrained from writing it, made no difference. Whether he went on with the diary, or whether he did not go on with it, made no difference. The Thought Police would get him just the same. He had committed—would still have committed, even if he had never set pen to paper—the essential crime that contained all others in itself. Thoughtcrime, they called it. Thoughtcrime was not a thing that could be concealed forever. You might dodge successfully for a while, even for years, but sooner or later they were bound to get you."[5]

"Nothing was your own," Orwell wrote, "except the few cubic centimeters inside your own skull."[6]

"Get Over It!"

Fortunately, Orwell's nightmare fantasy was just that—a fantasy. In reality, however, God does care about our thoughts. However, it's not in order to punish us, as did Orwell's Thought Police. Rather, the Lord cares about our thoughts because He wants to protect us from doing the kind of things that sooner or later, in one way or another, bring heartache and sorrow not only upon ourselves but on others as well (usually the ones we love).

The final commandment of the Ten reads: "You shall not covet your neighbor's house; you shall not covet your neighbor's wife, nor his male servant, nor his female servant, nor his ox, nor his donkey, nor anything that is your neighbor's" (Exodus 20:17).

If the ninth commandment took morality to another level (that of our words), this one goes even deeper—to our thoughts themselves. The commandments progress from actions to words to thoughts (God's got everything covered). The bottom line is that if you control what's in your head, taking charge of the rest of yourself will be relatively easy.

> What would be easier, and more likely to save you and others a lot of pain: to stop coveting your neighbor's spouse, or to terminate the affair after it has already taken a toll?

And talk about protection! If someone who does *not* lie is less likely to commit other sins, consider someone who doesn't think wrong thoughts. What would be easier, and more likely to save you and others a lot of pain: to stop coveting your neighbor's spouse, or to terminate the affair after it has already taken a toll?

The commandment does not read, *You shall not have desires or passions*. God created us as beings endowed with such things. To equate desire itself with longing for your neighbor's wife is to compare a man making love to his wife with one who solicits a child prostitute. The problem is with the objects of that desire, not with desire itself.

Who hasn't felt what a stranglehold envy can have on the soul? It can sweep over a person like a firestorm, burning and destroying everything else until all that's left is a painful frustration that dominates the charred remains. You can't be happy, satisfied, or at peace while envious. If not controlled or subdued, envy and covetousness of what others have will make your life miserable (who needs this book to tell anyone that?).

PREVENTING FOREST FIRES OF JEALOUSY

Of all the bad thoughts, why was coveting what's not ours singled out here? Blowing out a match the moment it ignites is much easier than putting out the forest fire. Think about how much human suffering and loss began in the desire for what wasn't one's to begin with. How many crimes, how many sins, how many lives have been ruined—all of which we could trace back, at their core, to a desire for what didn't belong to us?

Who hasn't felt envy's choking grip? Someone, somewhere, some "neighbor," is always going to have more or better than us, so the commandment is God's way of saying, "Get over it!" If not, those desires will roll over us, consuming and ruining us by leading us into places that we would never go if we could see the end from the beginning. Stories abound about how Larry Ellison, the multibillionaire founder and CEO of Oracle, burns with envy because Bill Gates is richer than he is and owns a bigger company. (In other words, here we have a multibillionaire jealous of someone else's money!)

Bill Gates

The grass always seems greener on the other side of the fence.

A fable tells about a man who received a special gift: whatever he wanted or even wished for would be his. Except for one caveat: whatever he got, his neighbor would get double. The man wished for a big house; his neighbor got one twice the size. When he desired a beautiful new horse, the neighbor received two beautiful horses. While he had everything he could want, he enjoyed none of it, because his neighbor always had more. The envy squeezed the life out of his guts until, unable to stand it anymore, he wished he could be blind in one eye.

In most printings of the Ten Commandments, the two bottom commandments, those upon which the whole law sits, are the fourth (the seventh-day Sabbath) and the tenth (the injunction against covetousness). Together they cover just about everything. God is our Creator. He made all things (John 1:1-3), and by observing the Sabbath, we acknowledge His sovereignty over everything in our lives, even our thoughts. And we acknowledge that He owns all things, including what's ours and what's our neighbor's as well.

If we faithfully honor those two commandments, we'll more faithfully keep all the others, greatly enriching our lives.

Two Principles

Of course, it's one thing to be told not to covet and quite another not to. Everyone can know what the Ten Commandments are, but obeying them, especially the one about envy, is another matter. Most don't have a problem not committing murder. *Not coveting something of our neighbor's, however . . . ?*

How can we control our thoughts in this area?

First, we can be grateful and thankful for what we already have. "Not that I speak in regard to need, for I have learned in whatever state I am, to be content: I know how to be abased, and I know how to abound. Everywhere and in all things I am learned both to be full and to be hungry, both to abound and to suffer need. I can do all things through Christ who strengthens me" (Philippians 4:11-13). "Let your conduct be without covetousness; be content with such things as you have. For He Himself has said, 'I will never leave you nor forsake you'" (Hebrews 13:5).

Sure, no matter what you have, someone else will have more of it. But whatever you have, many will have less. A man without shoes felt sorry for himself until he saw a man without feet . . . that kind of thing.

> **No matter what you have, someone else will have more of it. But whatever you have, many will have less.**

A story tells about the philosopher Diogenes, who was taking a bath when Alexander the Great approached him. Seeing the aged philosopher, the king asked him if there was anything that he, the great Alexander, could do for the old man. After all, as conqueror of the known world he could have given the poor philosopher just about anything his heart desired, because he, Alexander, controlled it all. Surely there was something out of his vast wealth and power he could offer Diogenes, who seemed to own nothing.

Glancing up at the great conqueror, Diogenes said, "Yes."

"What is that?" Alexander answered, ready to be very generous.

"Please step out of my sunlight."

Think about it.

Also, if the tenth commandment works at the level of our thoughts, then it's at that level that we have to deal with it. Someone who ogles pornography isn't going to have an easy time of it not coveting his neighbor's spouse, is he? If we are filling our minds with wrong things, then we will have wrong thoughts.

The battle of the mind has to take place at the level of the mind. We can't turn our brains off. Even when we sleep, sensations pour into our heads. The key is what we funnel through our senses. What we read, watch, and listen to will determine what we dwell on. It's that simple. "Finally, brethren, whatever things are true, whatever things are noble, whatever things are just, whatever things are pure, whatever things are lovely, whatever things are of good report, if there is any virtue and if there is anything praiseworthy—meditate on these things" (Philippians 4:8).

The more that people focus on worthwhile things, the less that they will think about coveting what's not theirs.

Someone once said that the key to living like Christ is to concentrate on Christ, particularly the closing scenes of His life. As we focus on His great sacrifice for us, His total self-surrender for the good of others, His willingness to suffer and die so that others may live, His forgiveness of His enemies, and His complete death to self—how could our lives remain the same?

The key to living like Christ is to concentrate on Christ.

They can't. By making Christ our example, we'll be too busy helping those who have less than we do to be envious of those who have more. Or, as Paul said: "Each of you should look not only to your own interests, but also to the interests of others. Your attitude should be the same as that of Christ Jesus: who, being in very nature God, did not consider equality with God something to be grasped, but made himself nothing, taking the very nature of a servant, being made in human likeness. And being found in appearance as a man, he humbled himself and became obedient to death—even death on a cross!" (Philippians 2:4-8).

> **The more people focus on worthwhile things, the less they will think about coveting what's not theirs.**

Those who, through God's strength, are looking out not only for themselves but also for others, even their "neighbor" (regardless of his or her possessions), are going to know the reality of Christ's promise: "If the Son makes you free, you shall be free indeed" (John 8:36), because—as anyone who has been there knows—envy's a miserable kind of bondage.

---

[1] http://www.orthodoxytoday.org/articles/NeuhausMoralProgress.php.

[2] Delmore Schwartz, *Screeno: Stories and Poems* (New York: New Directions, 2001), p. 41.

[3] Niccolò Machaivelli, *Eight Great Comedies* (New York: Mentor Books, 1963), p. 88.

[4] George Orwell, *1984* (New York: New American Library, 1949), pp. 6, 7.

[5] *Ibid.*, p. 19.

[6] *Ibid.*, p. 26.

16

THE SUM OF THE MATTER

INTENTIONS

wo days before World War I ended, Pablo Picasso, almost 40 years old, was shaving in the bathroom of the Hotel Lutetia in Paris when the phone rang. When he picked it up, he learned that his great friend, poet Guillaume Apollinaire, had died. Weakened by a head wound in the battlefield, Apollinaire had succumbed to the Spanish flu, which would end up killing more people than the war itself did.

Picasso looked up, the phone still

PUBLIC DOMAIN

A Pablo Picasso self-portrait

Life is not a chess game of purposeless and meaningless forces.

pressed against to the ear. "His terrified expression in the mirror shocked him," Arianna Huffington wrote, "and his instinctive, immediate response was to draw his self-portrait with that undisguised look of mortality he had seen staring back at him."[1] According to Huffington, Picasso kept that self-portrait a secret for many years, not wanting anyone to see what it recorded.

"For Picasso, who feared mortality as the single most horrifying fact of existence, the death, at the unnatural age of thirty-nine, of the man with whom he had so closely shared the last fourteen years of his life was an agonizing shock."[2]

Picasso is, of course, now gone too, even though his paintings and name live on. But what good does that do him, now that he's as dead as his buddy Apollinaire decades before? What good does life do anyone, really? If science is correct, then someday—either through the big crunch, the big freeze, or some cosmic catastrophe in between—not only all of Picasso's self-portraits but everyone who ever even saw any of his paintings, along with every other human being, will be for-

Carl Sagan with a model of the *Viking* lander.

ever destroyed, with nothing left of them, not even a memory.

No wonder Picasso "feared mortality as the single most horrifying fact of existence." Mortality eventually negates not only our existence but its *meaning* as well. If not even a memory of us remains, then our lives are indeed futile.

This pessimism makes sense, however, only if one accepts the premise, so succinctly expressed by Carl Sagan, that "the Cosmos is all that is or ever was or ever will be,"[3] the idea that it alone explains itself—without need of a Creator. In such a cosmos, "man's salvation comes," wrote Ralph Burhoe, "in bowing down before the majesty and glory of the magnificent program of evolving life in which we live and move and have our being."[4]

So we bow down before the "majesty and glory" of evolving life. And then what? Eternal death in a doomed universe?

Some salvation.

Also, the idea of the universe as somehow self-explanatory, that we can find its origin only in and from itself, makes about as much sense as believing that the origin of chess emerges from itself—that the rules of the game, the form of the pieces, and the squares on the board all arose from the materials alone. It's like believing that the plot, characters, and dialogue of *King Lear* developed out of the play itself with no need of a Shakespeare.

And if all that's rather implausible for a game or a drama, how much more so for the universe containing that game and drama?

No wonder, then, that many people find the scientific explanation of origins logically, spiritually, and *intellectually* unsatisfying.

In contrast, we have the position explored in this book, which is that far from our lives having been the result of the same uncaring and purposeless forces that will eventually destroy them, we're here because a loving Creator not only made us but promises us an eternal existence in a new and better world: "For behold, I create new heavens and a new earth: and the former shall not be remembered or come to mind" (Isaiah 65:17).

> The idea of the universe as somehow self-explanatory is like believing that the plot, characters, and dialogue of *King Lear* developed out of the play itself with no need of a Shakespeare.

MEANT TO BE HERE

We have promoted the view that instinctively most of us sense that we're not here by chance but were created for a purpose, that our lives have a goal and end in mind.

"For who is not certain," W. H. Auden wrote, "that he was meant to be?"[5]

> **Death is an aberration, no more intended for us than a crash is for a jetliner. We were *intended* to be eternal, and in that intention alone we find the purpose of our existence.**

We *were* meant to be, but only because God created us, and He created us to have eternal life as well. Otherwise, our lives have no meaning. How could they, if they vanish into nothingness? Death is an aberration, no more intended for us than a crash is for a jetliner. We were *intended* to be eternal, and in that intention alone we find the purpose of our existence. Only when that intent is restored can our purposes be as well.

And that's why Jesus came, to restore us to the eternity that God meant for us to have: "Since the children have flesh and blood, he too shared in their humanity so that by his death he might destroy him who holds the power of death—that is, the devil—and free those who all their lives were held in slavery by their fear of death" (Hebrews 2:14, 15, NIV).

And the divine intention is fully, and finally, consummated at the Second Coming. "For the Lord Himself will descend from heaven with a shout, with the voice of an archangel, and with the trumpet of God. And the dead in Christ will rise first" (1 Thessalonians 4:16).

THE CONCLUSION OF THE WHOLE MATTER

In the book of Genesis, after confronting Adam and Eve with their sin, the Lord said to the serpent, Satan: "And I will put enmity between you and the woman, and between your seed and her Seed; He shall bruise your head, and you shall bruise His heel" (Genesis 3:15).

With these cryptic words God revealed the fundamental manifestation of the great conflict between God and Satan (see chapter 10).

Hostility would exist between the devil and his seed, and the woman and hers. The woman (a "woman" would become a symbol for God's people in the Old Testament and the church in the New Testament), and her seed would be in a battle with Satan and his seed until the end of time. "And the dragon was enraged with the woman, and he went to make war with the rest of her offspring, who keep the commandments of God and have the testimony of Jesus Christ" (Revelation 12:17).

Look at the parallels between the first book of the Bible (Genesis) and the last (Revelation): Satan, the serpent (depicted in Revelation as a "dragon"), is in conflict—he "went to make war"—with the woman and the rest of her seed, God's faithful people. The elements of Genesis 3:15 (Satan, the woman and her seed, and the hostility between them) are also in Revelation, only now at the end of earth's history.

A new factor, however, appears. Revelation describes the woman's seed as they who "keep the commandments of God and have the testimony of Jesus Christ." Later on, as Scripture depicts the end-time issue of "the mark of the beast" (see Revelation 13; 14) it describes God's people as: "Here is the patience of the saints; here are they that keep the commandments of God and the faith of Jesus" (Revelation 14:12).

The two passages in Revelation offer identifying marks of God's faithful—they are followers of Jesus, and they obey God's commandments.

Interestingly, King Solomon, after musing on the meaninglessness of life apart from the Lord, summarized how God's people should live: "Let us hear the conclusion of the whole matter: Fear God, and keep his commandments: for this is the whole duty of man" (Ecclesiastes 12:13, KJV).

What does this mean?

> **The promise is that no matter how flawed we have been, no matter how sordid our past, His perfection covers us, and we stand before God as if we had never sinned.**

First, "fearing" God is an Old Testament way of expressing reverence and love for God, who is also Jesus (John 1:1-3). It's what it means to have faith in Christ, to accept Him as our Savior, who died for our sins and whose perfect life can be credited to ours through faith alone. The promise is that no matter how flawed we have been, no matter how sordid our past, His perfection covers us, and we stand before God as if we had never sinned. We stand before Him in His—God's!—own righteousness. "This righteousness from God comes through faith in Jesus Christ to all who believe. There is no difference" (Romans 3:22, NIV).

LIVING OUT RIGHTEOUSNESS

Then, because we are credited with the righteousness of God, we are to live out that righteousness, manifesting it through obedience to Him. And according to the Bible, we express such obedience by keeping the commandments of God—all of them. "For whoever shall keep the whole law, and yet stumble in one point, he is guilty of all. For He who said, 'Do not commit adultery,' said also, 'Do not murder.' Now if you do not commit adultery, but you do murder, you have become a transgressor of the law" (James 2:10, 11).

What James was saying is what the book of Revelation, in another context, also declares: we must have faith in Jesus as our Creator and Redeemer, and we reveal that faith through obeying the Ten Commandments.

Do you have a past that haunts you, a guilt that hangs over you, memories that stomp through your mind and give you no rest, not even while you sleep?

If so, what can you do?

First, you must surrender your own will to God by confessing your condition, and then claim through complete trust in Jesus a reward that you do not deserve but that God gives you anyway—the perfect righteousness of Jesus. Don't wait until you feel worthy or good enough. You are not, nor ever will be. If you were, or ever could be, then you wouldn't need a Savior and the gift He offers. But because you aren't and can't, Jesus came and paid the debt that you, in your unworthiness, owe but can never satisfy.

> **Jesus came and paid the debt that you, in your unworthiness, owe but can never satisfy.**

You must claim, then, for yourself, Jesus' righteousness. Accept it as your own. Take it because He offers it to you as a gift. Without it you will be left to stand on your own, with all your sins and past deeds to condemn you before a God who demands perfect holiness—the holiness that only Jesus Himself has but that He promises to all who come to Him in faith and repentance.

FINDING A COMMUNITY OF FAITH

If you have done this, or are still thinking about doing it, it's important for you to find a body of believers who can help you along with your journey of faith. Christianity is a communal religion. To be a follower of Jesus is to be a part of a body of fellow believers. People often rail against "organized" religion, yet what would they prefer—a "disorganized" one? There's no such thing as a one-man or one-woman Christianity, any more than there is a one-man or one-woman physics. As Christians, we must belong to a body of believers from whom we give and get support, encouragement, and fellowship.

Though different churches have many good, faithful, and devoted Christians who can help you in your spiritual quest, as you seek and pray for a community of support and fellowship, look for a few crucial points.

First and foremost, find a group that exalts Jesus. They must teach that He is God, that He died for your sins, and that only through faith in Him can you stand perfect and justified by God Himself. Look for a church that emphasizes Jesus and His death on the cross as central to everything they teach. Jesus crucified, Jesus condemned, Jesus risen must be the foundation of all their beliefs.

Inseparably tied to the death of Jesus at His first coming is the promise of His second. Locate a church that believes in and teaches about the Second Coming, because, as we've seen, without the Second Coming the first was useless. The dead are still dead, and will remain so until Christ returns. Hence, whatever community you find, they must be people awaiting the return of Jesus as the consummation of all their hopes in God.

And though many loving and good Christians believe that the righteous soar off to heaven at death while the lost endure torment for eternity in a boiling hole somewhere in the ground, you—having read this book—now know better. Only a firm, unwavering knowledge, based on the Bible and not on tradition or experience (for experience can be deceiving), of what happens to the dead will protect you from the numerous and often subtle New Age and spiritualistic deceptions that have tainted even churches. As long as you understand that the dead are in an unconscious sleep until Christ returns, you will never fall prey to such errors. How much better, therefore, to join with those who, like you, understand that the dead are asleep and unconscious, awaiting the coming of Jesus?

And, finally, from what we have studied all through this book, and especially from these verses in Revelation 12:17 and 14:12 that we have just looked at, you should choose a church that—while understanding that salvation is by grace alone—teaches that God's law still applies to our lives today. Join a group that teaches obedience to God's moral law, the Ten Commandments, as the way of showing our love to Him and of living out divine principles that can make our lives so much better here and now.

> **WHAT TO LOOK FOR**
>
> - Find a group that exalts Jesus.
> - Look for a church that emphasizes Jesus and His death on the cross as central to everything they teach.
> - Locate a church that believes in and teaches about the Second Coming.
> - Choose a church that teaches that God's law still applies to our lives today.
> - Don't settle for a church that downgrades the law, or any of the commandments.
> - Anyone searching for truth, no matter the cost, can find such a church.

Don't settle for a church that downgrades the law, or any of the commandments, including the seventh-day Sabbath, the one most commonly ignored. How ironic, for this is the one commandment that provides the foundation of all other Christian beliefs, because all other beliefs derive from the fact that God is our Creator, and the seventh-day Sabbath—embedded in creation at the Creation itself—remains the immutable and eternal sign of Creation, the doctrine upon which all else rests.

In the end, anyone searching for truth, no matter the cost, can find such a church. They *are* out there. And the good news is—You don't need to be an Einstein to find one (if a Goldstein could, anyone can!). God promises: "And you will seek Me and find Me, when you search for Me with all your heart" (Jeremiah 29:13).

And, as you search with all your heart, don't forget Clifford's

"It is always wrong, everywhere and for anyone, to believe anything upon insufficient evidence."

principle, either: "It is always wrong, everywhere and for anyone, to believe anything upon insufficient evidence." Clifford's right. It is always wrong to believe upon insufficient evidence. God gives us plenty of reasons and plenty of evidence to believe in Him and to rejoice in the "hope of eternal life which God, who cannot lie, promised before time began" (Titus 1:2).

---

[1] Arianna Stassinopoulous Huffington, *Picasso: Creator and Destroyer* (New York: Avon Books, 1988), p. 159.

[2] *Ibid.*

[3] In John Polkinghorne, *The Faith of a Physicist: Reflections of a Bottom-Up Thinker* (Minneapolis: Fortress Press, 1996), p. 9.

[4] In Polkinghorne, p. 63.

[5] W. H. Auden, "Talking to Myself," *Selected Poems* (New York: Vintage International, 1979), p. 297.

If you are interested in knowing more about this topic and other Bible-related issues:

- Visit **www.itiswritten.com** to view a weekly Bible study program online and use the free online Bible studies.

- Find answers to hundreds of Bible questions in 16 languages at **www.Bibleinfo.com.**

- Explore Bible lessons, games, and stories just for kids at **www.KidsBibleinfo.com.**

- Find more books on Bible-related topics at **www.reviewandherald.org.**

- Request Bible study guides by phone. Call 1-800-HIS-WORD (800-447-9673)

- Request Bible study guides by mail. Send your name and address to:
  DISCOVER
  It Is Written
  Box 0
  Thousand Oaks, CA 91359